C. H. P.

Coffee Has Priority

C. H. P.
Coffee Has Priority

*The Memoirs
of a
California Highway
Patrol Officer*

By Ed Marr
State Traffic Officer, Retired
9045

Christian Literature & Artwork
A BOLD TRUTH Publication

C.H.P. - Coffee Has Priority
Copyright © 2014 Ed Marr, Sr.

ISBN 13: 978-0-9904376-0-4

BOLD TRUTH PUBLISHING
PO Box 742
Sapulpa, Oklahoma 74067
www.BoldTruthPublishing.com
boldtruthpublishing@yahoo.com

I dedicate this book first to Almighty God
and to all law enforcement officers (those road warriors)
who are soldiers in God's Army
and to all those who shall become soldiers in the rank
and file of Heaven's military host.

Table of Contents

Chapter 1
Snatched From the Clutches of Death

"For the life of the flesh is in the blood…"
Leviticus 17:11

August 1983: I had just cleared the Days Inn Restaurant in South San Diego at 21:30 hours where I had been writing reports and sucking down my quota of Cups of Joe. I thought, my goodness, I sure feel jittery. I looked at my hands and they were trembling away as I made my way towards my patrol car. I thought, I could just kick myself for drinking all that coffee!

I looked skyward enjoying the warm, balmy breeze of the evening, taking in the smell of fresh air. Knowing it was nearing the end of my shift and three days off, I proceeded back to the barn to close out my eleventh consecutive work day, hoping that somewhere and some how South San Diego County would remain quiet as it had been throughout the day. I prayed to God that I could make it back to my area office without incident, when suddenly radio dispatch called me saying, 87-5. San Diego! I picked up the mike and answered, San Diego, 87-5, northbound I-5 approaching National City, go ahead! Dispatch: There's an (11-79) major injury, possible fatality collision northbound I-5 south of the Coronado Bay Bridge. I responded code 3 and within minutes I arrived first, being the closest unit. Notifying dispatch as being (10-97) at the scene, I quickly secured the collision scene within the north bound lanes of I-5 and requested additional assistance (tow trucks, coroner, paramedics and additional CHP units). Making a quick mental assessment of the scene, I went about creating my flare pattern from the rear (south bound) side of the collision scene, so as to forewarn on coming northbound traffic.

Some good Samaritans did stop along the shoulder of I-5 near the scene and ran out towards me offering their help. Now typically under normal conditions, such help would be refused however, given the precarious location of this collision in a darkened stretch of freeway and in a blind curve to approaching northbound vehicles, I accepted their assistance. In short order, additional units had arrived to maintain the rear guard and to protect those of us at the scene from approaching northbound traffic. At this time, I was able to further assess the scene. In the northbound number 2 and 3 traffic lanes, I saw Vehicle One (V-1). It was a green 1974 Mercury Monarch, on its wheels basically facing north. It had sustained massive rear end collision damage. I noticed Vehicle Two (V-2). It was a blue 1967 Mercury Montego that basically faced north and it was positioned on the unimproved right shoulder of I-5 at or near the collision scene. V-2 had sustained massive front end collision damage. The driver, an older man, was found seated in the left front seat of V-2 obviously expired. He had been impaled through the chest on the steering column and his upper body was positioned in and through the windshield.

Redirecting my attention to V-1, I walked around its right side in the darkness following the beam of my flashlight. I noticed a heavy red liquid on the pavement streaming from beneath V-1. Suspecting it to be transmission fluid, I walked on until I discovered to my horror the lower extremities of a person underneath V-1. I trained my flashlight on this person, and realized that this person seemed to be a woman and the liquid was not transmission fluid at all, but a copious amount of fatal blood! This person was face down on the pavement with nearly two tons of V-1 on top of her! As she laid there, her body twitched

2

(in the throws of death) and the sight and smell of her demise was evident! I instructed the good Samaritans to assist me flipping V-1 onto its right side, being careful not to slip in the large pool of blood. Having accomplished this, we all noticed that this person was in fact a young woman. She lay there on the pavement slowly loosing her life; (after all, life is in the blood).

Let me describe her injuries. As I said, this woman was found beneath V-1. Through the course of my investigation and the evidence available, it was obvious that she either was knocked down or thrown to the pavement upon impact with V-2, which caused V-1 to crash down on top of her little body. Her upper torso had been completely crushed as though she had been die-stamped into a mold with extreme weight of pressure! I mean, her entire upper half was completely flattened! From her head to her waist, she was as flat as my citation book! As for her head, her skin served as a bag wherein her skull fragments, brain, sinuses, eyes, etc. were contained! Standing by, all we could do was take note of her faint groans and watch this poor woman expire as we waited for the paramedics to arrive. Thanking these good Samaritans for their assistance, I instructed them to leave the area. In the meantime, I proceeded to complete my scene investigation. Through the scene evidence, I learned that this woman apparently was looking under the hood of V-1 after it had broken down in the northbound number 3 traffic lane. It was at this time that northbound V-2 plowed into the rear of V-1 at full freeway speed (65-70mph). This impact forced V-1 forward, swallowing this woman under the hood. She was spit out onto the pavement after having traveled several feet forward inside V-1's engine compartment. The evidence revealed that V-1 spun about vertically on its front bumper and then crashed down on top of this woman, who was now a pedestrian.

The paramedics did arrive shortly after I released the good

Samaritans. One of the paramedics approached me and requested that I drive the ambulance to the nearest hospital. I obeyed his request and informed the other CHP officers at the scene as well as radio dispatch of this. The paramedic stated, Believe it or not officer, we've got a faint pulse! So here I am, driving this meat wagon to Balboa Naval Hospital. Talk about bells and whistles! This vehicle had it all. So I flipped every toggle switch I saw on the instrument panel and we departed. Good thing it wasn't a computer! With all the switches I flipped, had this ambulance been a computer, we probably would have all been deleted from off the face of the earth! We had about a 10 minute drive before we arrived at Balboa Naval Hospital. I allowed my thoughts to wonder about my life as memories flashed through the vast theater of my mind...

My Esophagus and the Bad Penny

"When I was a child, I spake as a child, I understood as a child,
I thought as a child: but when I became a man,
I put away childish things."
I Corinthians 13:11

I recall mom and dad informing me a number of years ago of how they nearly lost me several times during the first four years of my life. As it turned out, my esophagus kept collapsing thereby suffocating me! Time and again as a blue baby, I was rushed to the hospital. My parents told me that my esophagus was stretched until it finally held fast. If that wasn't enough and sometime later, I had swallowed a penny and it lodged itself in my wind pipe often times choking me. I was brought to the hospital again and this bad penny was discovered and removed.

Growing up as a child in a hostile family environment was very unfortunate for mom, me and my siblings. Dad was an unloving parent to us kids as well as a two-timing husband to mom. As a youngster, I recall many times being awakened in the middle of the night by noise, and then coming down stairs watching dad play poker with his crony friends at the kitchen table, all of whom were very loud and drunk. On three occasions, I recall dad stating, Hey guys? Ya wanna see something funny? To which his poker buddies would all say, Sure Jack! Show us something funny! At which time dad did scoop me up in his arms and placed me inside the kitchen oven, slamming the oven door where I sat in a fetal position inside this darkened oven chamber, crying and listening to the laughter in the kitchen. But each time my mother would respond to my rescue and like a valiant warrior, she would successfully chase these riffraff from the house, dad included!

My life as a youngster was pock-marked with episodes of parental abuse and scorn, in that my dad seemingly enjoyed taking his frustrations out on me and the rest of my family! I mean, his slaps to my head would cause my head to sear in pain and his repeated scornful statements towards me caused me great disillusionment about myself and my purpose for living. For example, although my birth certificate identifies my name to be Edward William Marr, according to my dad, my name was either you Dumb s.o.b. or you are a Stupid s.o.b! I often recall him telling me that nobody wants to hear what I have to say or that I would never have anything important to say! In retrospect, I suppose the reason dear ole dad made such statements to me back then was because of my demonstrated ability in English class. You see, I am not the most gifted with regards to science or math, in that I did struggle big time with these throughout my youth. But when it came to English and Physical Education, I soared! I persistently got "As" in each class.

Knowing that I had a flare for writing, I had difficulty relating to others within my immediate family and to other classmates, no thanks to dear ole dad! This flare compelled me to experiment with other words, not usually associated with my typical manner to speech. Consequently, I withdrew myself from others and learned to cope with life, and contend with my destructive disposition in my self-imposed protective shell. Therefore, I basically grew up as an angry young man and very much alone.

Since my family environment was hostile and very dysfunctional, I looked ahead to the day of my High School graduation, as this event would allow me to escape and join the United States Marine Corps. So in May 1970, just three days after graduation, I headed for the Marine Corps Recruit Depot in Paris Island, South Carolina and after graduation, I indulged myself in whatever my carnal heart desired for the next 7 years! But even then, I struggled with this broken record my dad had installed into my brain housing group as a youngster. Namely that I was stupid, lacking any intelligence, and it was these haunts which caused me to shy away from people! I soon realized that although I could escape that which had become familiar to me, I could never flee from myself and all that junk within me! You see, because I was a very angry young man (like an abused animal), all I wanted to do was hurt people, just as my dad had hurt us!

As an example, one day in the mid sixties, I was in the back yard of our home in Langley Park, Maryland with my dog. I remember striking my dog repeatedly in a rage and for no apparent reason. I do recall feeling very much beside myself at this time and my dog just happened to be near, so I beat my dog mercilessly. When she shied away from my hostilities towards her, I would beat her all the more, for I expected her to endure this punishment, just as my dad expected each of us kids to do!

Another example occurred after I had completed my recruit

training. In late 1970, I was transferred to Memphis, Tennessee where I attended vocational schooling. The course of instruction consisted of a 6 month curriculum. Approximately 19 weeks into this class, my instructor handed to me a stack of documents to be distributed to my classmates. I started from the back row and proceeded to distribute these papers. When I stepped up to Private Charles L., he gazed at me and then abruptly slapped my hand away, causing me to drop the papers to the floor. So I stooped down to gather them. Charles L. then took this opportunity to lean towards me and he told me to my face just how stupid he thought I really was! Now, to appreciate the situation here, please know that I was the largest student and Charles L. was an obnoxious jerk, who was raised in the street gangs of Chicago, and for 19 weeks I was the brunt of his insults! I continued to distribute the papers and soon returned to my front row seat. Shortly after taking my seat, Charles L. approached me from my left and stuck his face into mine and stated, My God, you are one stupid S.O. B, Aren't you? To this remark, I snapped and by the numbers, and in a precise military manner, I smartly marred (Pardon the pun) his face with my 14 inch fist, breaking his jaw in 5 places! As you can imagine, this event created quite a stir in class and I was promptly arrested for assault and battery and taken forthwith! After several minutes (which seemed like hours) had passed by in isolation, I was surprised by my escort who took me to see the Master Sergeant, who was a large stately man, himself. The handcuffs were removed and TOP told me that all my classmates testified of Charles L's provocation towards me and of how long I endured his insults! Consequently, all charges were dropped and I was a free man!

I soon graduated and was transferred to MCAS Cherry Point, North Carolina. One Sunday morning, several weeks later, as I returned to my barracks from the Chow Hall, I saw Charles L. approach me from the opposite direction. Immediately, my thoughts grew apprehensive. I thought, I'll just do my best to avoid him. But to my amazement, he called out to me saying, PFC Marr! I would like to talk with you. We met and Charles L. informed me that I had broken his jaw in 5 places with that one punch and that for the next 6 weeks; he had to sip his food through a straw because his mouth had been wired shut. He went on too say, Ed, I was raised in the streets of Chicago and I had many run-ins with other gangs and the law. I've been involved with many fights, but I had never been hit like that! He said, Ed, I had a lot of time to think about my life there in the hospital, and I need to ask for your forgiveness, and I apologize for all the things I said about you. I accepted his apology. Shaking hands, we went our separate ways. I never saw Charles L. again.

Chapter 2

A Drill Instructor and a Divine Interruption By Way of a Collision

"The Lord shall laugh at him: for he seeth that his day is coming."
Psalm 37:13

I traveled the globe during the first four years of my enlistment having spent three years abroad on Embassy Duty, and during the last three years of my last enlistment, I served as a Drill Instructor at the Recruit Depot in San Diego. I was honorably discharged from the USMC on Thursday morning April 29, 1977. It was about 10:45 a.m. I headed home thinking, what in the world have I done! I mean, I had no job marketable skill to speak of. I had no friends. I had nothing to look forward to but an uncertain future! Preoccupied with these thoughts and stopped in eastbound traffic, I allowed my vehicle to rear end a VW van in front of me in the east bound lanes of University Blvd. and on the overpass of I-805. I stepped out of my car wearing my D.I. uniform and confronted the other driver. She reminded me of one of my old school teachers. I estimated her age to be about 40. (I was only 26.) She walked briskly towards me and stated, my son, are you alright? To which I replied, Lady! I am not your son and why in the @#$%^& did you back into me? She informed me that I struck her from behind and that she did not back into me. Well, this reality check really set this event in my life off the charts! So, to reacquire some degree of integrity, I insisted that we exchange our personal information and call the police. To this, she agreed. I also suggested that we clear the traffic lanes for our safety. Again she did agree. Funny thing is, the police never showed up for the length of time that we were there at this location.

Now, you must know that any collision generally draws a crowd of looky-loos, right? Well, this collision was no different. In fact, across the street, I recall seeing three fat grease monkeys wearing their tee shirts up and over their large, distended bellies laughing at me! From their perspective though, it must have been mighty humorous to see a long, tall, lanky Drill Instructor going at it with this little woman! I suppose, had I been in their shoes, I too would have laughed. Anyway, during the course of our contact, this woman kept calling me my son! I repeatedly told her, I was not your son and that you are not my mother! I told her, I knew what my mother looked like, and lady, you do not look anything like her! What's more, this woman stated, my son, I want to pray for you! Can you imagine that! A complete stranger wanting to pray for me! I told this woman, Look lady. I was raised a Catholic and I had been an altar boy. I told her, if you want to pray for me, just write my name in that black book of yours and you go your way and I'll go mine! I told her, I need to go home and soak my throat, if you know what I mean? In spite of my best efforts to discourage this pesky woman throughout our contact, and even after exchanging our personal info, she still insisted on praying for me!

Eventually, just as I was about to depart, she walked up to me and took my hands into hers and raised them up to her forehead! I thought this is just great! Here we were standing on the sidewalk in broad day light and in front of all these people! She closed her eyes and commenced to wail away in her claptrap prayer! I stood there demanding her to let go of me, but she would not! Time and again, I attempted to pull my hands free. (In hindsight, I suppose that if I really wanted to free myself, I would have done so with one mighty tug, but I didn't want to hurt this little woman; neither did I want to appear as a jerk.) Get it? Several minutes went by. I stood there picturing in my mind, this little person flailing about in the air in front of me with her death grip as I attempt to shake her off. I looked all around and saw all these people laughing at me! Now, this made me feel very uncomfortable, but for some reason, I calmed down and waited patiently for this gal to finish. Having overcome my awkward feelings, I began to listen to what she was saying and to whom she was speaking. I mean, this gal knew someone that I did not know! A few moments later, I allowed myself to seriously consider this new option that stood before me. So I bowed my head, and sensing this, she proceeded to lead me in what is known as a prayer of salvation. After completing this prayer, I felt something enter my head, flush throughout my entire body down to my toes, and then exit through my head in a flash! I stood there quaking in my boots! I asked her what had just happened and she just stood there laughing! She wasn't laughing at me, but she did laugh just the same as though she had a secret. Well, I haven't been the same since!

I had already applied for the California Highway Patrol prior to my discharge from the Marines. Having been discharged, I faced an uncertain future for myself, my wife and young daughter. As it turned out, I survived 10 months on unemployment checks, and other odd jobs. Eventually though, the CHP background investigator did contact me. In short, he basically said, Ed, the CHP needs men like you in uniform. However, unless you take care of these State taxes which you owe the State of Maryland, the CHP will not accept you! To this I said, Officer Steve, if you hire me, I'll pay the $600.00 I owe! He remarked, the CHP does not work that way. So pay it off as soon as you can. Otherwise you can forget about the CHP!

To appreciate this scenario, I had been struggling with the Maryland Tax Board for the previous three years. They sent me so many letters threatening me with this and that, that I just threw the letters away! I figured, well they can't get blood out of a turnip. However, I really had a desire to become a CHP Officer! So I asked Officer Steve to speak to the Tax Board on my behalf. He did so three separate times but with no positive results. Again and again, I continued to receive letters from the Tax Board. I grew more anxious with my current living conditions. So one Sunday morning, I turned on the television. The program that appeared on the tube was hosted by a man named, Oral Roberts. At the time, I had no clue who this man was. To me, he was just another television preacher asking for money! Anyway, I listened to what all he had to say. He talked about Seed Faith and that if I plant a seed of faith (money), Almighty God would honor that. Not having anything to plant, I followed his advice and prayed for the first time to this new God that I had encountered several months back. I stated, Lord God, you know that I want to become a CHP Officer. I promise you, that I will be your man in uniform if you would only speak to the Tax Board for me and cancel this debt, as I don't have the money to pay it off myself! I did not think anything more about it. About three weeks go by and I receive another Tax Board letter. It was no different than any of the others, which I had thrown away. But this particular letter, I did retain. In fact, I placed it on the mantle of the fireplace and there it remained for nearly an entire day. Later on that evening, having acquired the mind set to open the letter; I did so and began to read.

Dear Mr. Marr,

After reconsideration of your account with us and considering your desire to serve the State of California as a law enforcement officer, it is our decision for you to cancel your account. You are hereby given notice that your account with the State of Maryland has been abated as we do not wish to interfere with your future employment as a State Traffic Officer with the California Highway Patrol. But know this, in the future, should you ever return to the State of Maryland and take up residency here, you will be required by state law to pay state taxes. Good luck to you, sir.

Signed Maryland Tax Board

I was so excited about this letter; I could not believe it! I went to several of my neighbors, knocking on their front doors. I spoke with three of them and I asked them to read this letter aloud to me and to tell me just what all it meant! I specifically asked them to define the word, abated! Finally, reality set in and I knew right then and there that Almighty God had heard my prayer on that Sunday morning three weeks earlier! Needless to say, I contacted Officer Steve and informed him of this great news. I soon found myself going to CHP panel interviews, participating in physical strength testing as well as aptitude testing. As it is said, the rest is history.

Chapter 3
The Flight and My Probation Years

"And the Lord caused me to hear in mine ears..."
Isaiah 22:14

My flight to Sacramento, California was scheduled for the President's Day holiday weekend in February 1978. The carrier was the now defunct Pacific Southwest Airlines (PSA). While in flight heading north from San Diego, all was fine. The flight was full and people were settling in for this short hop to Sacramento. Several minutes into the flight and flying at 28,000 foot elevation, I heard somebody say to me, You will not go a full 20 years with the California Highway Patrol, but know this, that something will happen to you during the last half of the decade of the eighties that will separate you from your employment with the CHP! Now, I did not know anybody on this flight, and I certainly did not speak of my personal business with another. I abruptly looked over my shoulders to identify the person whose voice I had just heard. Not recognizing any specific person, I settled back into my seat once again and considered what I had just heard and experienced. Somehow, I intuitively knew that I just heard the very voice of God, audibly, and that for the very first time!

I graduated from the CHP academy in July, 1978. I was immediately transferred to the area office in El Cajon, California, where I was to commence my two year probation. While there, I met two influential officers, who would eventually impact my life and that for the rest of my living! Their names were Benny H. and Argus H. Now, there were three other officers who transferred to the El Cajon office along with me from the academy. Each of these men had the experience of working at least one fatal collision ahead of me. I would not work my first fatal collision for several weeks later and when I did, it would be a triple fatal involving seven vehicles. But until then, I struggled with the haunts of my past, which were a constant replay within my mind. (Thanks dad!) I was struggling with the person of my past and the development of this new person present. In short, I realized that over the years, I actually became two persons in one! The person of my past and the person of who I was present! I realized that the man I was in my emotional dysfunction (past) as well as my mental depravity (present) was greatly lacking in aptitude. By this I mean to say that I lacked the potential to acquire a specific skill pertaining to law enforcement duties, since I was also very slow in learning the ropes, even during the extra attention extended towards me by my superiors! My apparent deficiencies did not go unnoticed either! The other officers were complaining of my immaturity to one another as well as to my supervisors. Consequently, I was placed on remedial training, and this training primarily focused on my written documentations and my inability to communicate with other officers and the motoring public. In retrospect, I realize now that this probationary period was one of the most beneficial seasons in my life, and its rewards are still with me to this very day! You see, any probation serves to qualify, correct and to purge. Now, the word, probation speaks of a season of discipline. By this I mean to say that there is a process of time or a systematic procedure that must be successfully followed if the rookie (me) could ever hope to become a vested employee of the CHP. The intent was to prove my worth to the uniform and profession and to also expose those discrepancies within my character that could render me unsuitable and therefore possibly make me a discredit to the law enforcement profession.

During the most arduous weeks of this remedial training, it was the responsibility of my Field Training Officer(s) to critique every word that I intended to say and every thought that I had regarding the observed violations. Once I made the enforcement contact, I was then critiqued on my body language, whether I carried myself in such a way so as to intimidate. Being a large framed man in uniform, at least in this scenario, did not work towards my benefit, at least not then. I mean, any other shorter officer could get away with this or that, but for myself, I had to come to grips with the fact that anything that I did (no different from any other) would be an embellished perception or an exaggerated perspective by others. I felt so awkward and the pressure was on, for if I did not pass this remedial period, my employment would be terminated! Even my report writing abilities were scrutinized! I had no breathing room whatsoever! Talk about reading my mail, every single facet of my personhood as well as my character was under the proverbial microscope! But as I said previously, this probation period reaped its rewards that I still value to this very day. In fact, you are reading the results of this critique in that my critical thinking as well as my writing skills have become for me, a very important part of life.

I successfully completed my probationary period and I thank God for that! The skills that were imbedded into me soon revealed there benefit compared to the other officers. My report writing skills were fine tuned. I eventually introduced 3-D factual diagrams in many of my more involved collision investigations. I received many written compliments from insurance companies, from the courts as well as from those involved or who were related to their dearly departed. These accommodations became known in the area office and would follow me throughout my career, and my superiors showed their recognition of these on my annual evaluation, which varied from a 4 to a 5 (5 being the highest). Oftentimes, other officers would be challenged in their literary skills and occasionally they would vent their disapproval of me. I was often given the duty of reviewing the submitted reports of my fellow officers, and if needed, they had to correct them.

If there is any one particular truth that I can appreciate the most out of all this training is the following: When I place my name on any written document, others will read it, and whatever I have written is a direct reflection of the content of my character! You see, every man has a song to sing, whether that song is Godly or not; and it is that song which is outwardly expressed or demonstrated in our writings, our deeds and our words. Together, they all speak of the content of character, don't they? And when you think about this, such a truth is applicable in every area of life.

Now, as a spiritual application towards a relationship with Almighty God, you should know that all the days of a man's life, in the days and the time of his living are for each of us, our probationary period! It is God's intention that each and every one of us be reconciled to Him through the ministry of reconciliation (spiritual discipline) by way of His Word of Reconciliation! This will require intense scrutiny of every facet of your character, for your character denotes that which is within your soul, specifically pertaining to those things catered to within the vast expanse of your mind.

But speaking of time, let's consider for the time being, the time of our probation. We can either waste our time or we can choose to embrace it. Should we decide to embrace our probationary time then we will realize that the times in which we live are crucial times in deed and should a man pass his time away without giving himself the time of the day in which he lives, he shall be ignorant of his future time [his latter end] and shall experience another time to burn, for without probation, he literally kills time. Either way a man chooses, he shall experience for all eternity another time without end, because we are all eternal beings. How often it is said, how fast time passes by or how quickly time flies. Well, these adages are very applicable to the time of our probation, which is speeding by like chaff that is whirled away in the wind! Just look around at your own life and consider just how fast time, even the last decade has flown by! Truly, man's existence on earth is but a shadow, which appears for a very brief moment in time and then our time as human beings shall vanish!

C. H. P. - Coffee Has Priority

Chapter 4
An Honest Question that Clashed with a Denominational Perpective

"And think not that ye have Abraham as your father:"
Matthew 3:9

In the previous chapter, I spoke of two men who would later influence my life, they were Officers Benny H. and Argus H. One Friday night, I hooked a late drunk driver. Having already performed my duties out on the beat, I returned to the barn, where I met Officer Benny. He too had a late report to write. It was now about 2200 hours. Both of us completed our reports and decided to sit a spell and chew the fat. Now, you must know that to the rest of the officers in the El Cajon office, Officers Benny and Argus were considered to be Jesus freaks. In fact, I was told by several to avoid these two altogether. Well, Benny and I spoke of many things. But we ended up speaking of the Bible and his relationship with Almighty God. I was truly touched with what all Benny said. So I asked him to help me with my own personal walk with God. He led me in a prayer of rededication and from that night on, Officer Benny did disciple me for several months and that on a weekly basis. Specifically, he taught me through the use of several Bible study workbooks, which were printed by the Navigator Publishers. Once a week, I met Benny at his home, driving some 10 miles out of my way for this instruction in righteousness. You see, I became very hungry and for me, this was my pursuit after righteousness! Where before, I never read books (other than a comic book from time to time) I now found myself quenching this new found passion for inspirational books. (Over the years, my personal library has changed from the basic reading to more in-depth literary works). I quickly purchased a Scofield Bible, KJV. This Bible soon became part of my law enforcement equipment along with the tools of the trade, which I either drove or wore around my waist. Where before, all I had was a revolver and a baton, as my primary and secondary weapons, I now had a Sword and a double edged one at that. And in time, I would learn that this Sword would become my primary weapon of choice!

I could not put the Bible down! Even on the job, I would find time to read and study God's Holy Word. At home, I regularly commenced my day with a very early quite time, which often lasted for several hours. I kept a daily journal, and soon I had accumulated several legal pads! This practice in turn, would eventually lead me to begin writing thematic studies. From here the Spirit of God compelled me to write manuscripts. And with the literary skills that I had acquired during my probationary period, I was able to investigate Scripture and not just merely study. I learned early on that to study referred to academic purposes, such as for an exam, but when I investigated Scripture, I did so with the intent on getting to the truth. After all, this was in keeping with my investigations, to get to the root cause of a matter.

Well, Benny and I eventually came to an impasse during our weekly Bible studies. Specifically, with regards to this concept of tongue talking, and a reference out of 1 Corinthians 13:8-13; 14:2. I asked Benny for his take was on these passages. He said, Ed, the literal translation of the King James Version was intended. I, on the other hand, had another notion which pertained more to Jesus Christ, of whom the Bible does speak of. But what really dissolved our Bible Study was the question I had regarding speaking in tongues. Benny said, Ed, this practice was probably essential back then, but is no longer relevant for us today. I asked him to convince me of this, and to qualify his argument in Scripture. He could not, so I basically challenged his erroneous theology, when I said, Benny, could it be that you are mistaken and that you should not believe everything your denominational dogma or doctrine says? Benny, based upon my own research, it seems that the Word of God has been tampered with in many areas by men for their own purposes. This then would render the written Scripture as fallible, wouldn't it?

Now, nobody likes to be told that he or she is wrong, but to Benny, it was like telling him that he was stupid or an ignoramus! Because of this issue, he surmised that we were no longer compatible and he abruptly ended our study! This hurt me deeply. From that time on, Benny and I worked together but our relationship had dwindled and grew very cold, and all because of an honest question, which clashed with a denominational perspective!

Up and Over

So I preoccupied myself with work as well as my own pursuits in God's precious Word. I had mentioned Officer Argus H. Now, Argus was a very quiet man. He only spoke when spoken to. Rarely did he carry on a conversation with anybody. All of the officers thought him to be rather odd, more so than Benny. Consequently, they either avoided him or made fun of him. Imagine that, grown men, brothers in arms, heckling one of their own! Anyway, in time, I submitted a transfer request, as I desired to work in the San Diego area office, which was only twenty miles from my home. So on January 3rd 1980, my transfer took place.

Once again, I found myself being trained. Only this time, my training was more of an overall area orientation, so as to acquire a lay of the land, so to speak. Having transferred to the San Diego area office gave me a feeling of a new lease on life, a do over. Whatever mistakes and whatever reputation I acquired back in El Cajon, would be left behind, or so I thought. I figured, since I was in a new venue, I would have plenty of opportunities to reinvent myself.

Knowing that one of my strong suits was my writing ability, I was already aware of the fact that San Diego was a much larger metro area than El Cajon, and so I knew that I would be very busy with more reports and investigations. I intentionally chose to work the south end of San Diego County, since I resided in the South Bay area. But I also knew my decision to work the south end would require responding to calls which concerned activities from the United States-Mexico Port of Entry in San Ysidro, Calif., and in time, I would spend most of my shift there, writing extensive arrest reports.

During the first week in my new home office, I was assigned to work the graveyard shift. One night, it had been raining and as usual, collisions were happening throughout the area. My partner and I responded to a collision which had occurred within the northbound lanes of the I-805 Freeway and on the bridge span over I-8. Upon our arrival, each of us set out to stabilize the collision scene, knowing that other emergency agencies were in route. My particular task was to obtain the measurements and other cross triangulations of the vehicles involved for the factual diagram, which I would prepare for the collision investigation. Now, this bridge span is 250 feet above I-8. The collision occurred after midnight. The rain was pouring down, but in spite of these adverse conditions, we all performed our duties to the very best of our abilities. Having said this, picture me, if you can, pacing off the measurements from the point of impact and walking towards the east bridge rail in the rain. I was so engrossed with what I was doing, I actually forgot where I was! When I reached the east bridge rail, my forward momentum carried me over the top when I stubbed the base of the rail with my right boot! Up and Over I went! To save myself from immediate death, I dropped all that I had in my hands and falling, I caught myself on the bridge rail by hooking the top of this rail with my two arms! There I was upside down, legs straight up and looking 250 feet down into the darkness of certain death! Because of this darkness, no other officer could see my precarious situation, so I had to leverage my legs, kicking them back over the rail, if I were to save my own life. I struggled to do so, and accomplishing this, I lowered myself into the standing water on the roadway, where I sat and swallowed my heart and regained my professional composure—after all, I was a professional CHP Officer! Although I was soaked through and through, I completed my assignment, only to be asked by my graveyard partner, where have you been and what ever happened to you? I just ignored him and we headed back to the office for a clean uniform.

A New Transferee

Now, several weeks went by and I learned that the area office would be receiving some new transferees. One of these was identified as Officer Argus H! When I first learned of his transfer, I became alarmed for some unknown reason. In April 1980, Argus H. and the others did arrive and his arrival particularly caused me greater anxiety, and I had no idea why! As it turned out, Argus was assigned the wall locker next to mine. After several days of avoidance, I confronted Argus stating, Argus, ever since I first learned that you would be transferring to San Diego, I was gripped with anxiety, and since you have been here these last several days, I've had to avoid you at all costs! Now, I have no reason for fear, and yet I do! Argus, why is this so?" Argus, in his usual quiet manner, simply said, "Ed, it's the convicting power of the Holy Ghost. Have you been going to church?" My immediate response was, "No I haven't, but what does that have to do with anything?" Argus said, Ed, you and I need to talk. I want to invite you to meet me at the Morris Cerullo World Evangelism Headquarters at the El Cortez Center downtown at your leisure. Argus went on to say that his wife worked there as the Executive Secretary and that he was well known and accepted at the ministry headquarters. I told Argus he would be waiting a long time before I would ever set foot in a place like that!

Chapter 5
God's Tornado

"Out of the south cometh the whirlwind...And it is turned round about by his counsels: that they may do whatsoever he commandeth them upon the face of the earth. He causeth it to come whether for correction, or for his land, or for mercy."
Job 37:9-13

I never forgot his invitation. In fact, Argus often invited me to attend church services with him, especially when he was the guest speaker. Eventually though, I did accept his invitation to meet him at the ministry headquarters. So, on a Thursday morning in late January 1981 (on my day off) I did appear at 10:00 am, having just cleared the San Diego Municipal Court House on an earlier summons. Argus presented himself to me and escorted me throughout the ministry complex. I met all the employees, and they all made me feel truly welcomed.

Argus took me to the penthouse located on the roof of this high rise building. He escorted me into the office which was identified as the, I Care Center. Now, this office had a glass wall, which faced southwest overlooking the San Diego Bay. It was a large viewing pane of lightly tinted blue glass. The view it provided of the Bay from this elevation was absolutely beautiful! I thought, if this were my office, how difficult it would be for me to concentrate on work if I had a view such as this! Argus introduced me to his friend, named John S., who was the center's director.

Now, I had my reservations about this visit. I mean, I had already determined to vacate the premises, if I felt challenged or in any way threatened! Knowing ahead of time that I would be stopping by, and knowing something about this ministry, I did prepare three pages of spiritual questions about God, speaking in tongues, apostles and prophets, healings, etc. and I had them with me in hand. So I presented these questions to both Argus and John, and to my wonderful surprise, they answered every question authoritatively to my satisfaction, so much so that I was no longer apprehensive about my visit. Now, I lost track of time. I looked at the clock and it was now approaching 1400 hours! I told both men that I needed to get back home. Before I left, Argus stopped me and John asked, Ed, would like to receive the Baptism of the Holy Ghost? This was the one question that I did not want to hear! Sensing that I was very uncomfortable about this, Argus and John assured me that I was not in any danger. In fact, they even challenged my masculinity just to get my goat. Not being one to turn away from a challenge, I accepted their gracious but dubious offer.

Stepping away from John's desk, the three of us assumed a standing posture of prayer, while grasping each others hands. (Actually, they grabbed mine.) Suddenly, both men raised their hands and mine skyward and each bellowed out in this nonsensical gibberish. I stood there laughing at the two of them and remarking, why does God need to hear this? Surly, He understands English? They ignored me, if in fact they ever heard me to begin with. After several minutes of listening to their deafening tongue, and as I stood between them, I looked over the San Diego Bay in front of me. My mind brought me back to my collision in which that woman prayed me through. So I stood there, waiting patiently for Argus and John to finish their little demonstration of foolishness. Showing no immediate signs of ending, I stated to them both, look, I am larger and stronger than both of you put together! If you do anything to knock me off my feet or pull the carpet out from under me, I'll know right then that this is a bunch of bunk and that it is not truly of God! Well, I no sooner finished saying this when I noticed something odd appear in the sky above the San Diego Bay Bridge. Concentrating on this USO (Unfamiliar Spiritual Object) I was struck with fear! I thought, Aha! These guys lied to me! They assured me that I would not be in any danger! So, what in the world was this thing descending from above the clouds? I mean, this USO was in the form of a long shaft of spiraling wind. It originated far into space beyond the blue sky! It slowly descended from the sky and curved ever so gently towards the El Cortez Center! It passed through the clouds and over the Coronado Bay Bridge and headed straight for the penthouse! By this time, I was highly agitated and very much concerned for my personal safety. This thing appeared to be a rope tornado! So, I closed my eyes tightly and assumed a defiant position of advantage! I stood between Argus and John. I shouted, Okay God! If this is really you, then you will have to knock me off my feet! I opened my eyes just as I saw this whirlwind enter the room from the southwest corner of the ceiling. This wind lapped the room and with every lap, it lowered towards the floor, thickening as it descended. I watched this take place and it appeared to me that the three of us were inside the eye of this vortex! I fought with all my might to remain standing, bracing myself as best I could.

When I came too, I found myself on the floor some ten feet from where we were all standing. In fact, the three of us were lying on top of an overturned metal bar lock cabinet, in the threshold of the office doorway and up against a large heavy desk! I awakened to a host of people, who had flooded the room and each one had placed their hands on me and all were praying aloud in their tongue! I was weak and somewhat bewildered! After a few minutes, I stood up and asked what had happened. John and Argus told me the following: Ed, you were standing between us straining under some force! Whatever you saw, it really had you on edge! Suddenly, both your legs were raised to your front and you were suspended in mid air between us for a moment; and then you were literally picked up and thrown up and backward, taking us with you! Your head struck the wall just beneath the ceiling and above the cabinet. You came crashing down on to the cabinet, knocking it over and against the desk. You along with the furniture were pushed across the door entry where you came to rest. What's more Ed; you took Argus and me with you and that is why we were on the floor with you. Suddenly, I was the talk of the ministry! I then proceeded to inform them of my unique God encounter, which only fueled the excitement of the hour! I immediately bellowed out some Holy Ghost inspired prayer. To which another said, we have a diamond in the rough standing here with us! Even Morris Cerullo was advised of this supernatural event.

Before I left for home, I spoke a prayer on behalf of my first wife, Mary. In essence, I requested that the Spirit of God would some how speak to her while she was at work. The time was now 14:45 hours. I arrived home just ahead of her. She looked at me as if I were different. I certainly felt so. While we made up the bed, I asked her whether something odd occurred with her while at work. She hesitantly said, you will probably think that I am crazy, but yes, I did have something happen to me. Why do you ask? I urged her to continue on, so she related that while she sat there at her assembly line table working, she heard some man call out her name. She looked up and said, yes. Looking around, she noticed that everyone was attentively doing their job. So she figured that she just imagined hearing a voice. A few moments later, she heard some man call out her name once again, but this time with more volume. She again replied, yes. I'm over here! Once again, everybody was busy at their assigned tasks. Mary said that this time, she was truly frightened. Redirecting her attention to her work, she once again heard this man call out her name even louder than before! Upon hearing this, she retired to the woman's rest room and sought refuge in a toilet stall. Being alone there, she heard that voice one more time, but this time it was soft and gentle. As she spoke of her experience, I was doing my very best to contain myself, for I knew that Almighty God answered my prayer! So, I informed Mary of what had happened with me earlier in the day. She just looked at me as if I had just pulled some kind of trick on her, which she did not appreciate.

Days later, I was invited to attend a ministry banquet. During the festivities, I observed John and Argus speak to Brother Morris Cerullo at length of our unique tornado experience. I was introduced to Brother Cerullo and we spoke for a few minutes and I was all the more received and accepted by one and all.

Nothing, Nothing, Nothing, POW!

Days went by. I could not but notice that there was something different taking place within me and about be. I mean, I became consciously aware of the fact that I possessed a new found boldness to witness like I have never ever had before! Whereas, I was a closet Christian at best previously, I now found myself boldly testifying and being used of God while on the job. Lost souls were an easy prey for me. I felt like a lion on the prowl stalking my intended prey, for in my predatorial mind, everyone was prey! I was leading ten, twenty, thirty, and fifty… per week and month after month to the Lord! I found myself compelled to pray for many injured motorists, most of whom were healed of their bone crushing injuries! I encountered several demonic entities as well as angelic hosts in my patrol vehicle, at home, at crime scenes and at collision scenes, and all this as a direct result or after math of that tornado! Through the next several months, I realized that the Almighty was more God out on the highways and hedges than he was in church! These close encounters had a profound affect on me. My mind began to change, bolstering my Scriptural investigations. I soon perceived a major deficit within the church house, namely that the power and the anointing of God were absent, and yet out where the rubber meets the road, He could be found! These encounters challenged my marriage not that God would have me divorce my wife, but that she might embrace Him along with me. But as it turned out, she refused to do so and years later my marriage did end.

Chapter 6

The Demon of Murder, "Red" and Eight Smurfs

"From whence come wars and fightings among you? come they not hence, even of your own lusts that war in your members?"
James 4:1

A few weeks pass by, and while on routine patrol and traveling north on SR-163 from downtown San Diego, I happened upon a white ministry van. Its external identification revealed that this vehicle belonged to the Morris Cerullo World Evangelism. So I followed it for several miles. The reason I did so was simply to obtain reading material from the ministry's School of Ministry. You see, I had learned during my visit to the ministry headquarters that damaged reading material was regularly donated to prisons. So my thought was that perhaps I might obtain a book. I followed the van as it pulled into the ministry warehouse. The driver stepped out noticeably concerned. I asked him if I could speak to the manager. He introduced me to a middle aged woman named Marilyn. I asked her if they had any damaged books that were intended for the prisons. Marilyn then stated, Officer Marr! The Lord has just commanded me to tell you that I was not to give you any damaged material. But that I was to give you brand new material. In fact, He instructed me to provide for you all the workbooks and all the required reading material of the School of Ministry! And Officer Marr, the Lord would have me to tell you that He charges you to learn this material and then to instruct others! Do you understand this?

I was truly humbled by this generosity, and I vowed to Marilyn and to Almighty God that I would learn this material to the best of my ability. I departed with several boxes, knowing that Almighty God had just graduated me into a new level of investigation.

Since there are so many encounters, I just can't recall there exact order of occurrence. So, I suppose the earliest encounter occurred during the graveyard shift. My partner and I were both fellow cadets in the CHP academy. Upon graduation, Officer Jim M. was transferred to one of the Los Angeles area offices, while I was transferred to El Cajon, approximately 40 miles east of San Diego. I had mentioned previously that the San Diego area office received a few transferees, two of which were Officers Argus H. and Jim M. As it turned out, Jim M. was partnered with me on the graveyard shift. One night, as we were on patrol of I-805 in the north end of our jurisdiction, we exited the free-way at the Sorrento Valley exit. At this time in the early 1980s, all that existed at or near the southbound and the northbound exits were car pool parking lots. On the east side of I-805, there was a berm line which paralleled the freeway running north and south. Between this berm line and the freeway was positioned one of the carpool parking lots. As Jim and I exited the freeway, we observed several San Diego P.D. squad cars parked in a row with head lights directed in one unified direction. We drove on over to have a look see. As we made our approach, we spotted what appeared to be a body bag draped over a corpse, which apparently had been reported to that agency. After contacting the SDPD at the scene, I walked on over to have a closer look. I stooped down near the head and shoulders of this body. I picked up the towel that covered the head, only to discover that this in-dividual had his face blown off with a possible shotgun! I placed the towel back and I questioned why? In fact, I asked Almighty God a question. I asked, Lord, I've worked fatalities due to colli-sions, but this is a murder. Father, is there a difference between a murder and the loss of life due to a collision? After all, death is death, is it not? Immediately, as I remained there with this corpse, I did hear loud and large laughter, only this laughter was not from a party. It was the laughter of one. So I looked up and turned east towards the direction of this laughter. I aimed my flashlight towards the direction of this laughter and just beyond the bermline, there appeared a huge demon! This thing rose in height. It was as large as King Kong! This demon stood there gloating over this body. Its head was that of a bull, horns and all and its tongue was long and tapered at the tip! Its eyes were aglow with the fires from the very pit of hell! Its body was that of a muscular man and covered in hair. He looked every bit the part of an evil cartoon figure. Well, I became nauseous and I retreated to my patrol vehicle backing as I went. I never took my eyes of this huge demon. It stood there nodding its head in approval. His arms were either folded across his huge chest or they were moved to the hip with his hands placed there, assuming a position of authority. When I reached my vehicle, Jim and another officer noticed my complexion. Jim said, My God, Ed! You look like you have just seen a ghost! Are you alright? To this statement I responded, Jim! You believe in God don't you? Jim said that he did. I said, Jim, you believe that there is a real devil, don't you? When Jim answered that he did, I grabbed him by his arm and pointed at this demon, which was still visible, at least to me. I said, Jim, look! Jim apparently could not see this demon. He must have thought that I flipped out! I told Jim, Let's get out of here! But Jim wanted to stay. I told him, Jim, I'm feeling sick, let's leave. Jim thought I lost it. Realizing this, I grabbed him and literally threw him into the patrol car and I drove off quickly. I headed south on I-805, flooring it! Poor Jim! He just looked at me in amazement! I'm sure that he felt endangered by my bizarre behavior. After traveling a considerable distance, I pulled over, white knuckles and all. I told Jim what all I observed, but since he did not or could not see the demon, he disbelieved me.

Well, this event was the start of our divorce, so far as Jim and I were concerned. We were split up a few weeks later.

In the late spring of 1987, I responded to a vehicle fire near the L street exit off I-805. Upon my arrival, a station wagon was fully engulfed in flames. The South Bay Fire Department had arrived ahead of me and they were busy dowsing the flames. I was introduced to the owner/driver of the vehicle. Now, I thought I was a tall figure of a man. This fellow stood nearly 7 foot tall! He was a young black gentleman. His hair (afro) was red with streaks running through it from front to back. My first words to him were, Red, I'll bet that you are some kind of a musician, aren't you? Surprised by my question, this man said, As a matter of fact officer, I am. I play the guitar with a band called the Reds. But how did you know that? I told him, Partner, let's just say that your hair gave you away. With the fire out, we both walked over to the smoldering station wagon. I looked into the cargo hold and spotted a Dungeons and Dragons book. On the cover appeared the caricature of the demon I saw gloating over the dead body, previously mentioned. So I reached in and took this book and I told Red of this demonic encounter. He said, oh yes! The demon's name is-----------. He is the demon of murder! Upon hearing this, I was filled with an eerie chill that ran up and down my spine! Because of our engaging conversation, I offered to take Red home once we cleared the scene. He lived in the community of Imperial Beach, which was about a 20 minute drive south. While in route, we spoke of the demonic world, which led into a discussion of the spiritual world. Since I did not have much time, I knew that this was a divine appointment and connection. So I urged Red to come to faith in Jesus Christ and accept Him as his personal Lord and Savior. Red accepted my exhortation; so I led him in a prayer of salvation, right there in the front seat of my patrol vehicle! What's more, I prayed that he would receive the Baptism of the Holy Ghost and immediately, he began to speak in other tongues! Now, that is what I call a two for one baptism! We arrived at his home. He lived in an apartment building. He pleaded with me to remain in the parking lot, while he went upstairs to tell his mother and other family members of his salvation. Before I knew it, out came his entire family and they all ran down to greet me! Talk about excited! These people were shouting praises to Almighty God and doing a Holy Ghost jig all around me! After several minutes, I had to leave, but before I did, Red's mother and all the rest of the family either gave me a big hug, a thank you or a kiss.

Eight Little Smurfs

One night while working the south end and on the second shift, Radio dispatch instructed me to respond to the U.S.-Mexico Port of Entry for a hostile deuce arrest. When I arrived, I could not believe what I saw! Beneath the canopy in the parking lot on the American side, I watched eight Immigration Officials push a large white male adult around one to another within a circle. As I approached this uniformed mobocracy, I overheard many of these officers heckling this irate and distraught man. I broke into the center of this circle and chided every one of these officers for their unprofessional conduct and behavior. I then turned to this very agitated man and backing him up against a pillar I said to him, Mister, if you don't calm down or if you cause me any reason to be concerned for my personal safety, I will take you down! Do you understand? He complied and I was able to make an arrest for DUI without incident. While en route to the San Diego Jail, my prisoner wept bitterly for most of the trip. He informed me that he was a decorated Vietnam Vet, who had experienced some hellacious combat during his tour of duty. I informed him that I too was a Vietnam Vet. Immediately, I sensed that his incensed disposition was attributed to Post Vietnam Stress Syndrome. So I spoke with him from this common ground. I told him, Sir, although I was in the Nam for two years, I never served any time in the bush as you, which means I never dug a fox hole. However, don't let that disappoint you, for you see, I am in a war zone right here and now! And tonight, you and I are foxhole buddies! Having said this, I arrested his attention and before we arrived at the jail, another soldier had enlisted into God's army! Hallelujah!

Chapter 7

O God! Book 1, Book 2, Book 3 and Then Some

"Call now-is there any who will answer you?
And to which of the holy [angels] will you turn?"
Job 5:1 AMP

I start with what I have identified as Oh God! Late in our shift, my beat partner, Al Wilkerson and I were heading back to the barn. While we were both headed north on I-805 from the Port of Entry, we both received a dispatch call which directed us to respond to a situation involving shots fired that concerned a disabled motorist on I-805 at the Paradise Valley Road exit. Al and I were nearly 10 miles south of this particular location, so it would take us several minutes to arrive. While in route, radio dispatch informed us that there were two parties (men) involved. One was seen running north in the center divider from that location bare-chested, swinging his shirt frantically over his head and the other ran into the darkness up the exit ramp. Upon hearing this, I instructed Al to take the ramp and that I would head north along the left shoulder. I inadvertently passed my man, since it was so dark in this particular area of I-805. So I pulled over immediately and stepped out of my squad car ahead of him. This little fellow stopped abruptly about 30 feet from me and turned about and ran south! Now, the department does not pay me enough to take off running after someone, so I got back into my vehicle and floored it north to the nearest center divide turn around. I then headed south, with spot lights on. I came upon this man, who was most definitely very much out of control! As soon as I drove up to him, He turned about and then headed north once again! I backed up and attempted to calm this man down verbally. All I could hear was Oh God! O God! O God!

Finally, I managed to talk this Philippino man down from his panic stricken state of mind. He told me what all had occurred. He related to me the following: My friend and I were in my small station wagon traveling north on I-805 when it began to sputter. I took the exit just as my car stopped running. I believed that I had run out of fuel. Initially, I parked under the street light on the ramp and there we waited for the CHP. As we waited for a patrol unit, another vehicle drove up and stopped behind us. Two men stepped out and offered to help. The driver suggested that he push the station wagon further down the ramp, out of sight and into the darkness. This way he said, nobody would tamper with us or my car. So, I took him up on his offer and he pushed my car into the darkness. We all got out and I expect-ed a friendly situation. But the driver pulls out a hand gun and pointed it at my friend and me. We immediately panicked and ran in separate directions. All I know is that I heard shots fired! I don't know whether this guy shot at me or my friend.

I spoke with Al car to car. I advised him of the situation and asked him if he found the other man. He replied that he had not. Meanwhile, this man with me kept repeating Oh God! So, being a Holy Ghost stalker, I said, Sir, I could not help but no-tice what you have been saying. He replied, what do you mean, Officer? I explained, Sir, ever since our first contact, I've heard you shout Oh God repeatedly. I went on too say, Sir, now I am not God, but He did send me here in direct response to your call! I said, Sir, I'll bet that you are a Roman Catholic or perhaps an Episcopalian, right? He said, what does that matter to you? I said, Sir, with all do respect, I never heard you cry out to your priest. You never called out for your pastor or your nun. Neither did you call out for your deacon or elder! You called out to Almighty God alone! Now, why did you do that? He paused for a moment and said, because I was scared for my life! That's why Officer! So I pressed the issue and said to him, Sir, God was fully aware of all that had happened and that although He did not intend on this, He did use it to get your attention. I am here in direct response to your need, and as I said, I am not God but He is mighty within me. His heart's desire is for you to open your heart and let Him into yours!

Having said all this, I knew that I had arrested his attention. (Pardon the pun.) So I extended my hand towards him as a gesture of friendship, to which he accepted. I then proceeded to engage his mind with the following witnessing technique. I immediately pulled my hand away from him exclaiming, what are you doing? He looked at me with surprise. So I extended my hand to him once again. He again shook my hand. Once again, I abruptly withdrew my hand asking, why did you take my hand? To which he said, I don't understand? Because Officer, I thought you offered it to me in friendship, I suppose? I informed him that he was correct, so I extended my hand one last time and as he took my hand into his, I simply asked, Sir, did you have to think about it, before you decided to shake my hand? Did you have to get all gussied up before you felt qualified or worthy to take my hand? Saying no to each question, I then said, Sir, Almighty God to whom you called out to, is here right now. I am not God, but He is very large within me, and it is His hand that you have taken into yours, for you see, just as you did not have to prepare yourself ahead of time before shaking my hand, neither do you have to clean yourself up before taking His. All you have to do is take His hand in yours, just as you are! Reminding him of his near death predicament, I proceeded to lead this man in a prayer of salvation. It was a wonderful encounter with God!

I then transported this man off the freeway and to a restaurant, where he was able to make a phone call and obtain a ride home.

And then there was the encounter with a young motorcyclist. It was a week day morning in heavy commute traffic on northbound I-5. Traffic was stop and go the entire length of the freeway, from San Diego south to the border. I was on routine patrol on I-5 in the Chula Vista Area, when I spotted a motorcycle passing all traffic on the right shoulder between the two overpasses of 'J" street and "H" street. I immediately pursued this bike and pulled the rider over without incident, south of "H". The rider took off his helmet, and as I approached, he said, Brother Ed! Well good morning to you. Did I do something wrong? Recognizing him from church, I requested his credentials of identification. He said, Ed, you are not going to give me a ticket are you? After all, we go to the same church! To this remark I said, Look brother, my allegiance is not to you, nor to the church, but to my job and the motoring public. What's more, Almighty God wants you to know that I probably just saved your life or that of another! Sign here please! Realizing that he was not successful with his ruse, he became very angered with me and signed the ticket. Now, in order to appreciate this contact all the more, I would have you to know that this young man, named Kenny, never has ever given me the time of day whenever we met at church, and then to pull this stunt with me in his attempt to appeal to my better side, it just irritated me all the more! But should you think that if I had had a better relationship with this man, I would have let him off with a verbal warning, I can only say that every enforcement stop is hinged on the discretion of the officer; but most likely not.

Then there was the time I responded to a traffic collision on northbound SR-15 at the Ocean View Blvd. exit. It was a late morning collision that involved a single vehicle and some public property (A traffic sign). The vehicle was occupied by a middle aged man and a young woman (not his daughter). He was a married man and an intoxicated police officer! This man poured it on! He patronized me so much that I wanted to slap the drunk out of him just to shut him up! I did arrest him for DUI. He became highly irate with me, because I slapped the cuffs on him! I told him, As professional law enforcement officers, we can not live double standard lives. We are expected to abide by the same laws that we enforce, and that also includes our marriage vows! I'm sure his wife was not pleased with my report. Oh well, such is life in the fast lane!

C. H. P. - Coffee Has Priority

Chapter 8
Open Heart Message and a Cold Hard Floor

"He who is loose and slack in his work is brother to him who is a destroyer and he who does not use his endeavors to heal himself is brother to him who commits suicide."
Proverbs 18:9 AMP

I was assigned to work the overlap shift one quarter in the early eighties, and in this capacity I overlapped the morning shift and the afternoon shift, primarily to take up the slack between shift changes. Well, during the last half of my shift, I received a call of a collision that involved a pedestrian which did occur on I-5 beneath the 30 foot high pedestrian overpass in up town San Diego. Upon my arrival, I found a young woman who had apparently jumped off the overpass onto the freeway below. According to witness statements, this woman seemed to have broken her ankles and wrists upon landing on the pavement. Failing to kill herself, she struggled to crawl out of the traffic lane when she was struck by a northbound Datsun 280 Z. This impact scooped her high into the air and she once again landed in the traffic lane, gravely injured. The paramedics arrived in short order and having stabilized her, immediately transported her to the County Hospital, where I would meet her later. I completed my collision scene responsibilities and proceeded to the hospital. While driving, I suspected that this woman probably had died while in route, so I anticipated a simple follow-up for my collision investigation. However, when I arrived and as I walked into the cubicle in the ER, I collapsed to the floor! You see, the medics hinged her chest cavity wide open, like a large door and while seated upright in the gurney, the doctor performed open heart message! By this I mean, the doctor was pumping this woman's heart with his right hand, just as I walked in! When I saw this, I instantly collapsed to the floor! You see, it is one thing to see blood and body parts out on the beat. But it is entirely different when I am around these anatomical elements in a clean sterile environment such as a hospital. Other medics responded to assist me off the floor. They gave me smelling salts and as I came to, it was strongly suggested that I avoid going back into this cubicle. However, I had a job to do; so I reentered and again my knees buckled and I fell out of the room! I decided right then that I would wait for the hospital staff to provide me the personal information about this woman at their convenience. Meanwhile as I waited, the Holy Ghost whispered into my ear saying, Son, just as this doctor held this woman's heart in his hand, so too do I hold the heart of all humanity in mine!

The Hostile Amputee

*Wherefore He is able also to save them to the uttermost
that come unto God by him, seeing he ever liveth
to make intercession for them."
Hebrews 7:25*

One night, I just happened to be in the ER at the Chula Vista Hospital on "H" street conducting some accident follow up for a collision investigation, when I heard the hostilities of another patient, who had just entered the ER. The place was packed with the injured on all sides. After several minutes of listening to this hostile drunkard, one of the doctors ran towards me requesting my immediate assistance. Now, I had some things to consider. My options were, 1) I could attempt to apprehend this large, belligerent man on my own and risk disturbing the other patients. 2) I could some how lead this man outside, where I could take him down. 3) I could call my mommy! What I did not consider was that this man followed the doctor to the small room where I was in the company with several other accident victims, who were all stretched out on hospital gurneys, themselves. I observed that this irate man was bleeding profusely from his left hand, which was wrapped in a blood soaked tee shirt! He was accompanied by a very apologetic friend, who had in his possession a small white box that contained all four fingers belonging to this drunk! This amputee severed the fingers of his left hand using a circular saw at home while intoxicated. (Not a good idea). His friend, being very much aware of the commotion his drunken buddy was creating, could only apologize, and that he did often. This drunk confronted me nose to nose speaking all manner of vulgarities at me, while standing in the threshhold of the door to this hospital room. I decided on option 2 above, which meant that I had to risk a fight with this man in close quarters. But fortunately he never laid a hand on me. Since he did not cause any damage, and since he refused treatment for his injury, I permitted him to depart. After all, there is no law against stupidity or foolishness! His friend escorted this drunk back to their vehicle in the back parking lot. Before they stepped into their vehicle, the friend shouted to me saying, Officer, Officer! Please forgive my friend for his conduct! He has been going through a lot lately. He does not know what he is doing! Officer, Officer! Please forgive my friend for his conduct! As fired up as I was internally for battle, the Holy Ghost whispered in my ear saying, Son, just as this man interceded on behalf of his friend, so too do I plead on your behalf before My Father! Upon hearing his plea, I realized that Jesus Christ is ever interceding for me, with the same sincerity and intensity! In other words, Jesus does not merely say, Father forgive Ed! Rather, He is speaking passionate prayers on my behalf!

C. H. P. - Coffee Has Priority
Like a Dangling Participle

I had just received a brand new patrol vehicle. It was delivered to the office during my day off. Ideally, nobody else was allowed to drive this unit unless they were assigned to it along with me, for I had been designated car captain of this new chariot. I really looked forward to breaking this new unit in. With much anticipation, I looked forward to cleaning and waxing this new chariot of mine and removing all the brand new insects that came with it! After all, this was one of the few perks afforded us by the department, at the local level.

The next work day, I arrived for duty and suited up for my afternoon shift. It had been raining all morning, so the collision count was up, county wide. Due to the in climate weather, all of us officers knew that we were in for a busy day. Anyway, because of the rain, people were crashing everywhere, even crashing into squad cars! It was for this reason why my new vehicle was not in the lot upon my arrival. Immediately, as soon as we were suited up, all officers hit the road. My beat was I-8 in Mission Valley. As soon as I left the back lot, I was instructed to assist another officer with another collision on the connector ramp from I-8 eastbound to northbound I-805. Upon my arrival, I found that this other officer had my new chariot! As we tended to these collisions, on this elevated ramp, another vehicle spun out of control on the ramp and slammed into the rear of my new sled! This impact pushed the unit into my fellow officer pinning him between the unit's right side and the bridge rail. I immediately ran back to assist him and found him dangling over the rail with his right leg pinned by the unit against the bridge rail. He was in much pain and very concerned for his life. I notified radio dispatch and requested the tow truck and the paramedics. Upon their arrival, he was extricated from his dangling inverted position and taken to the local hospital.

Several hours later, I had the opportunity to visit this officer in the hospital. He informed me that many other officers had paid him a visit ahead of me. I said to him, well, that is fine because God saved the best for last! This officer said, look Marr, you're not going to preach at me are you?

To this remark I said, well, it is up to you! I can simply pay you a nice little visit and I tell you, if there is anything I can do for you, (and not really mean it) and leave. I for one will feel better for having done the very least, and you will be left here in pain and immobilized. The choice is yours. But if you do not want to remain bed ridden, then I can help you rise up out of this bed. Officer, what shall it be? Seeing my Bible in hand, this officer permitted me to speak Scripture over him. Having completed my visit, and having asked Almighty God to heal his wounds, I said my good-byes and left.

I arrived to work the next day, not expecting anything unusual and as usual. As I walked into the back door of the office, I was met by this officer! He was all lit up. Where yesterday he was hospitalized with his leg in an inflatable splint, he now stood before me jumping up and down and in full uniform! Excitedly, he said, Ed, you spoke Scripture over me, I felt electricity enter my body accompanied with intense heat. The heat radiated from my injured right leg and spread from there throughout my entire body. I was healed of my injuries! The doctors could not imagine what all happened, so they released me last night several hours after you left. Unfortunately, this officer never made a commitment for Christ, in spite of his healing. Sadly, his employment with the CHP was terminated several months later.

Chapter 9
Officer M and a Personal Challenge

*"For John truly baptized with water; but ye shall be baptized
with the Holy Ghost not many days hence."*
Acts 1:5

One fine day in 1983, I was loaded with reports which I had
to tidy up, before I could take on any others. So I remained at
the office, while all the other road warriors hit their respective
beats. Officer Al was one of these warriors and together he and
I patrolled the South Bay. Well, since I remained behind, Al was
the lone unit down on the south end of San Diego County. So, I
rushed as best I could to finish up these reports. When I finally
did leave the office, I expected to be notified by radio dispatch
of any activity, which is expected in a large metro area as San
Diego. But to my surprise, things were very quiet. So I contacted
Al, car to car, and requested a lunch break with him at the Days
Inn Restaurant (our usual watering hole). Al informed me that
he was already there and had been speaking with a Chula Vista
P.D. Officer. Upon my arrival, I met Al and this CVPD Officer
who identified himself as Officer M. Al informed me that he and
Officer M had been speaking of the things of God, especially of
the baptism of the Holy Ghost. Officer M was intrigued by this
conversation, and expressed a desire to receive this baptism. Al
told Officer M that they would have to wait for me to arrive.

Having been apprised of this, I sensed some apprehension
from Officer M. So I appealed to his masculinity daring him to
receive. I said to him, since Jesus Christ is willingly to give, my
friend are you willing to receive? Officer M accepted my chal-

lenge and the three of us left the restaurant and drove our patrol units to the dead end of northbound Bay Street. We corralled our units and standing between them just past twilight, I positioned Officer M between Al and myself. Facing each other, I reassured Officer M to trust us and to trust God for this spiritual event. I told Al that we were not to touch Officer M, but that the three of us would raise our hands and pray. Before to long, Al became very excited and began doing a Holy Ghost jig. (Either it was that or he had to use the restroom real bad!) Suddenly, Officer M was forced backward and was knocked to the pavement on his kiester lying prostrate before Al and myself! We both stepped towards Officer M and assisted him to his feet. I asked him what he experienced. He said, Well, Ed, neither you nor Al touched me; but as you were praying, it was like I saw a man step between both of you from behind. And this man stretched out his arms and punched me in my chest, knocking me down. Wow! I've never had such an experience like this before! From our previous conversation in the restaurant, I knew that Officer M was a devout Catholic and I also knew that this would definitely conflict with his theological assumptions. All we could do for Officer M from this point on would be to encourage him along the way in the days and weeks ahead.

From a Wheel Chair to a Table

"So Me-phibo-sheth dwelt in Jerusalem: for he did eat continually at the king's table; and was lame on both his feet."
2 Samuel 9:13

On another occasion in 1984, I worked the morning shift and while on routine patrol and traveling north on SR-163 from downtown San Diego, I received a call that there was an occupied wheelchair in the southbound traffic lanes of I-5, south of the Coronado Bay Bridge. Since it was my beat, it was my call and knowing the traffic conditions at this mid morning hour, I could only pray that whoever was in this wheelchair would not be killed. I arrived in the vicinity and saw no wheelchair. So I continued south on I-5 obtaining a visual of the connector ramps to and from the bridge. Again, there was no wheelchair. Moments later, I came upon very slow moving congested traffic. I passed traffic on the right shoulder, (this is legal when in performance of official duties!) Clearing the traffic to the front of the pack, I spotted the occupied wheelchair traveling south in the center lane! I drove ahead of the wheelchair and stopped my unit directly ahead of it. I stepped out and waited to tackle this guy, as he rolled passed me. The rider in this chair braked hard and spun to the right of my unit avoiding me altogether! So I hurried back into my patrol unit and pursued after this wheelchair! Can you picture this? Here I was running code 3 and traveling approx. 5-10 miles per hour in hot pursuit of an occupied wheelchair! I'm sure many of the motorists directly behind me thought the sight of this to be rather humorous. Here I was following (chasing) this chair, with all my equipment on. (My overhead patrol lights, my wigwag headlights and my siren.) But the occupant would not yield right! So I spoke to him via my public address system. Infuriating the rider, he spins abruptly about and heads directly into the slow moving traffic behind me. I jammed my unit into park and bailed out after him. Catching up to him, I dove for the chair and basically tackled it and its rider in the traffic lanes, tearing my uniform in the process!

The rider struggled to get away from me. I certainly had my hands full. This paraplegic began punching me in my chest and face, as I wheeled him on to the right shoulder. As to my patrol vehicle, another Officer did drive up during the course of this hostile scenario and he did reposition my unit on to the right shoulder for me. This paraplegic shouted, Let me die! Let me die! To which I immediately replied, Mister, you are one crazy fool! (Now, that is how you make friends and influence enemies!) This young man identified himself as Manuel H. I told him that he had a full life ahead of him. He replied, that is easy for you to say! You're not a prisoner of a wheelchair! I paused for a moment and then said, Manuel, your problem is not the wheelchair, but it's your heart! He asked me to explain. I said, Manuel, you have a heart issue that is more urgent than your physical condition and that Jesus Christ had full knowledge of all that has occurred in your young life. Furthermore, Manuel today can be your day of deliverance from your imprisoned heart. I asked Manuel how it came to be that he was chair bound. He said, when I was 2 years of age, I was accidentally shot by my older brother, who found dad's revolver, and ever since I've had numerous unsuccessful operations to restore my spine. I've been carrying hatred and unforgiveness towards my brother ever since. I responded and said, Manuel, it was your hatred and unforgiveness that has become a root of bitterness within your soul and that you could get rid of it today. Manuel would you like to continue to live this way and remain the same or would like to be set free from your torment? Manuel requested freedom. So, I prayed over him at this point and then led him in a prayer of repentance, to which he had to vocalize his forgiveness to his brother. I then led him in another prayer of faith. During the course of these two prayers, the other officer there just watched on in amazement! Although he never said squat to me about it, I could not but sense that this encounter made an impact within his heart, as well. Manuel broke down in tears, for I knew that the Spirit of God was dealing with him. Immediately, Manuel's visage changed! Both of us knew that he had been changed, for he had just been born again! I said, Manuel just as you were born into this world physically, likewise, you have just been born again spiritually into God through Jesus Christ His Son! Welcome home my brother!

Because of Manuel's extenuating circumstances, I went the

extra mile and helped get him established in a church. On those Sundays that I had off, I did pick him up at his home and took him to church with me. I did this for several weeks and was successful in leading his entire family to God! He eventually did marry a beautiful God fearing lady and the last I heard, they were doing fine, and he was dining at the Lord's Table continually!

C. H. P. - Coffee Has Priority

Chapter 10
Abominations that be Done in the Midst

"And the Lord said unto him, Go through the midst of the city, through the midst of Jerusalem, and set a mark upon the foreheads of the men that sigh and that cry for all the abominations that be done in the midst thereof."
Ezekiel 9:4

One fine day while attending court, I was seated in a crowded courtroom when I overheard two people sitting behind me conversing. By the content of their speaking, I determined that they were both attorneys. On this particular morning, there was a lengthy court calendar, so the wait was very long. As we all waited, I overheard these two attorneys discussing the Swearing In Oath. The woman asked the gentleman beside her, Why is it necessary to raise the right hand when swearing in? Her companion could not answer this question, so they dropped it. I however, could not just leave it that, so I turned around and informed them both that I overheard their conversation about the oath and I offered this explanation: I said, The reason why we are required to raise out right hand is because the right hand represents truth. Specifically, it is a symbolic gesture on our part that we as witnesses speak the gospel truth as opposed to perjury. Also, in the Scripture, Jesus Christ says of Himself that He is the Way, the Truth and the Life and that He is presently seated at the right hand of His Father. This explanation seemingly made an impact within them, for they just sat there looking at me dumbfounded.

On another occasion, while working the north end of San

Diego, I received a request for a roadside meet from another CHP officer. This officer (Chuck) was of Irish descent and a devoted Roman Catholic. We met out on the beat and Officer Chuck stated, Marr, what is with you? You're different from the rest of us (officers). I mean, you don't swear. You don't drink. You don't fool around. Why is that? So I asked, Chuck, what was your real concern? I asked him, what is it to you whether I do this or not do that? I spend most of my free time alone on the job. You and the other officers don't bother to befriend me. The only time you call upon me is when you are in need of help. So why the concern now, Chuck? Upon hearing this, Chuck became humbled and said, Ed, I've been watching you and I have to tell you that I have been very troubled of late by it, and I don't know why! I told Chuck, the Holy Ghost was convicting your heart, and that you are a marked man for Almighty God would have you to accept His Son Jesus Christ as your Lord and Savior. So Chuck allowed me to pray for him and over him. He accepted Jesus Christ and was brought to tears in his patrol vehicle. I cautioned Chuck to prepare himself for the inevitable. Specifically of the mind games he would experience denouncing his born again experience. I also cautioned him about his religious traditions and erroneous denominational doctrines. Even so, Chuck departed a saved soul!

Now Bob was a motorist whom I had the pleasure of meeting one morning in Chula Vista. I had just entered I-5 southbound from the "J" street on ramp. As I entered the freeway, I saw a large beige colored Oldsmobile convertible pass by at high rate of speed. I took off after it and paced it at 85mph and it was pulling away. So I pulled the vehicle over along the right shoulder just north of "E" street and confronted the one occupant. A black man, Bob was well dressed and looking somewhat forlorn. I obtained his personal credentials and stepped back to my patrol car to write the citation. Moments later, Bob walked up to me and began to speak. He related that he was a Navy man and was stationed at the 32nd Naval Base. He said that his wife had filed for divorce and he had just left the court-house. Feeling abandoned, he headed home and that is why he was speeding. So he begged me not to scratch out a citation for this moving violation, as he had enough going on in his life right then.

Now some time ago, I learned to listen to the still small voice of God when dealing with the motoring public and as Bob spoke, I was already moved with compassion towards him. So after Bob completed his explanation, I said, Bob, you are highly upset, aren't you? He said, wouldn't you be if you just left family court? I said, it would be remiss of me to allow you to continue on from this point knowing your present state of mind. So forget that I am a law enforcement officer and let's talk brother to brother, friend to friend and man to man. The reason why I say this Bob is be-cause you are as a ticking time bomb, waiting to explode and so to protect you from yourself and to protect others from you, let's talk. So we spoke awhile and I talked him down. I said to him, you know Bob, although you are going through this divorce, you don't have to go through it alone. I know a friend who loves you in spite of your mess. Would you like to know this man? Bob said, yes and so I took his hands in mine and introduced him to the person of Jesus Christ. Now the day was the usual Southern California day, beautiful! As I prayed over him, I looked up. I no-ticed the beam of a bright light shining upon and around our two vehicles, as though it were a high powered spot light! This light was brighter than the sun! Amazed by this, I looked up into this beam of light skyward. It seemed to have originated high above the clouds. Redirecting my attention back on Bob, who by this time had collapsed to his knees crying, I proceeded to lead him in a prayer of salvation. Bob completed the prayer and he was so overcome with the love of God that he could not even stand.

After several minutes, he regained his composure and stood up a new man! I explained to him that he was born again spiritually and that he needed to hook up with a spiritually healthy church. Bob thanked me and gave me a big hug before he departed for home. Oh by the way. Bob signed the ticket and even thanked me for it!

Early on, after I received the Baptism of the Holy Ghost, I experienced a season of travail. At the time though, I did not know this, since so much of all that I was encountering with God was all brand new to me. I recall that one day in 1982, I could not stop crying! In the natural, I did not have any reason to cry, but nonetheless I wept continuously, especially on the beat. Picture in your mind, this 275 pound CHP officer weeping during an enforcement contact with you. You would probably think either this guy is going through some serious situation in his own life, or that he was sorry for having stopped you.

For weeks, I could not stop weeping, and it didn't matter what I was doing on the beat! I wrote tickets, crying. I hooked and booked 300 pound bad guys, weeping! I investigated collisions, lamenting! After awhile, the Lord did bring to my attention why I wept as I did. In Scripture, there is an account of several men travailing publicly in the city streets of Jerusalem for all the abominations of its citizens round about within the city. Upon learning of this, I had a knowing of the purpose for my tears. Specifically, for all manner of abominations which Almighty God sees within the hearts and lives of the citizens of San Diego particularly, but also of this entire Nation!

Chapter 11
Entertaining Angels, but Very Much Aware!

"Behold, I send my angel before thee, to keep thee in the way, and to bring thee to the place which I have prepared."
Exodus 23:20

Our Angelic Ride Along

During my 12 year career as a law enforcement officer, I have encountered angelic visitations on four different occasions. I suppose the first occasion took place on a Friday night, when I was working the graveyard shift with my good friend "Ficky-Wicky". He and I were like two peas in a pod, which means that we clicked! Together, we were a force not to be reckoned with. Together, we were a very good team! We had fun, did our job to the very best of our abilities and racked up some very impressive numbers. Anyway, one night Ficky-Wicky was at the wheel and while traveling on I-8 eastbound through Mission Valley, a speeding motorcyclist passed us by. So we pulled behind him and attempted to affect a traffic stop. However, this rider had other intentions! (I tell ya, some people just don't want to cooperate!) The pursuit was on! We pursued this red 500cc Enduro motorcycle up Texas Street and then through the business district at speeds in excess of 85 mph. Since I was riding shot gun, it was my responsibility to keep radio dispatch appraised of our location, but also to communicate with Ficky-Wicky while driving. By this I mean that I reminded him of the basic EVOC instructions which we both learned in the academy. Such terms like, brake-fade, vehicle position, apex of the curve, space cushion, weight transfer, etc. were very useful expressions to remember while involved in any pursuit.

Well, during the course of this prolonged pursuit, I felt some-thing resting on my right shoulder. I recall reaching up swiping my hand across the top of my shoulder, and thought nothing more about it. A few moments later, I felt this same thing on my shoulder. So again, I reached up and swiped my hand across my shoulder. Again I felt this something on my shoulder. Now mind you, we are seriously engaged in this pursuit! I'm holding the microphone in my right hand and trying to hang on with my left as we rocket through intersections and catching air as we go! It was a wild ride! So, after feeling this something on my shoulder, I immediately intuited that we were not alone! So I looked over my left shoulder towards the back seat and there I saw another seated in the back seat of the patrol car, hitching a ride! I could not see his features distinctly, although I did see his form. He sat there and looked straight at me and waved at me with his right hand. I noticed that his left hand was extended towards Ficky-Wicky. It appeared that our passenger hitched a ride in the back seat of our patrol car while we were involved in a pursuit. Go figure! So I turned back around and asked Ficky–Wicky, the following question: Do you feel something on your left shoulder? Ficky-Wicky replied, what? What kind of a ques-tion is that, Ed? I said, never mind, you're doing fine.

We continued to chase after this bozo and followed him into the crowded parking lot of an amusement park across town. By now, the San Diego Police were involved in this pursuit along with us and since we were in their jurisdiction, Ficky-Wicky and I backed off our primary pursuit position, allowing them to take over. We trailed behind the SDPD units and as we en-tered this parking lot I told Ficky-Wicky to turn hard left and then make an immediate right around several parked vehicles. By doing this, we were in an excellent position to block the mo-torcyclist's escape. Sure enough, while the other P.D. units were chasing after the motorcycle, we found ourselves facing the motorcycle head-on! The rider began to swerve side to side across the pavement and between the columns of parked vehicles as it approached us at about 50 mph. with the PD units following! I told Ficky-Wicky to continue to roll but slow to a near stop. As we slowed, and just as the motorcycle came upon us, I grabbed the steering wheel turning it. This action caused our headlights to rock, confusing the rider. It worked, because his motorcycle crashed head-on into our patrol unit! The rider was thrown onto the hood of our unit crashing into the windshield! This impact forced shards of glass into my face and my eyes. The rider then rolled off the hood and dropped out of sight to my right. Assuming that our rider was on the pavement beside the right front wheel, I took my time getting out of the car. But Ficky-Wicky left the car in hot foot pursuit, saying Ed, he's over here! Come On!

Now, I am not the fastest man on foot! It took me quite a distance to catch up with my partner. We chased this man across a street and as we did so, a SDPD unit attempted to cut the man off by jumping the curb ahead of him and blocking the sidewalk with his unit. To our amazement, this guy hurtled the entire width of the vehicle! We chased this rider down a pitch black alley. This rider was 6'-4" young and fast! We managed to close the gap between us. I took out my PR-24 baton and threw it at the rider's feet hoping to trip him. But the baton fell short and bounced into his back. Feeling this, this rabbit poured it on and simply out ran us. Disheartened, Ficky-Wicky and I ended our chase and returned to our unit, which was left wide open and damaged. Ficky-Wicky and I surmised that since we did not have a body to justify my injury and the wrecked patrol car, our shift supervisor would have a field day chewing us out!

As we walked back to our wrecked unit, we hear a voice out of the darkness saying, Hello Chippies! I've got a gift for you!

We stopped and waited for whoever to make their appearance from out of the darkness. Sure enough, a SDPD officer ran our rabbit down tackling him. This gift was so much appreciated! So we took custody of our rabbit and escorted him back to our unit. Our supervisor had already arrived, waiting for us. While in our supervisor's vehicle, I conducted a brief interrogation for the arrest report. I asked our rabbit why he ran from us. He said, I've seen police pursuits on television so many times. I thought I'd give it a try for myself! I asked him, well, what do you think? Did you enjoy your little charade? He said, No sir! This was the dumbest thing I've ever done in my life! I'll never do this again. As to our unexpected angelic ride along, I never saw him again. I did however; receive accolades from radio dispatch for my precise communications with them throughout this pursuit.

Some time in 1984, I was off duty and performing some "honey do" assignments for my wife. I had just finished my tasks and walked into the house and as I placed my house keys up, I glanced into the master bedroom, just to my right. I spotted a little gray hairless fellow, wearing a gray prison jump suit sitting on my bed! This little imp looked up at me weeping. I noticed that his face had been disfigured. His countenance seemed to convey his abandoned existence. I simply looked at this imp and commanded him to get out of my home and to never return. Reluctantly, this imp scooted off my bed and walked through the perimeter wall of my house. I stepped into the kitchen where my wife was preparing a meal. She looked at me saying, My God Ed! Did you see a ghost? I explained what I had just seen and she shrugged it off saying that I needed to see a shrink!

One night I was invited to attend a Full Gospel Business Men's Fellowship International business meeting. There were approximately 20 men in all and since I was a relatively new member, I remained quiet, but enjoying the company of all just the same. As time went by, the discussion became more involved, as there were pros and cons on both sides of the table. Sitting across from me was a brother, who in my estimation was the source of the predominant pessimism. I looked up at him and wouldn't you know it? Perched on his back, I saw a hideous gargoyle gloating over the cynicism that had filled the minds of all these men. Immediately, I arrested everyone's attention when I spoke to Mister Negativity across from me saying, Brother, I have been sitting here listening to all your negative comments about this and that. I feel it my duty to tell you that right now you are the source of the problem! What's more, you are the host of an uninvited guest! He looked at me with a complete loss of thought. I said, Men, there is a gargoyle perched on this man's back. Its claws are dug deep into the back of our brother. So I stood up and simply commanded that foul spirit to depart. When it did, the atmosphere changed immediately for the better. Our brother apologized for his comments and related that his marriage was deteriorating and that this was most likely the reason for his demeanor.

MARINE CORP.

Graduating Series Staff Platoon 1073, Oct. 1976.
(I'm on the 3rd row from the top, 2nd from the left)

SGT. E. W. MARR   SSGT. W. L. BOSSAERT   SGT. D. L. HENDRICKS
GRADUATED 6 OCTOBER 1976

Our graduating Platoon 1074 Oct. 1976.
(I'm the Drill Instructor on the front row left)

California Highway Patrol

Statue and fountains in front of CHP Academy, Sacramento, CA.

Academy training on a steel catwalk 350' above
the San Diego Bay under the Coronado Bay Bridge.

CHP Academy Graduation photograph
1977

Here on a lunch break with my daughter Jaime
on top of my 1980 Dodge Patrol Car

Officer Marr caught on camera writing a traffic citation.

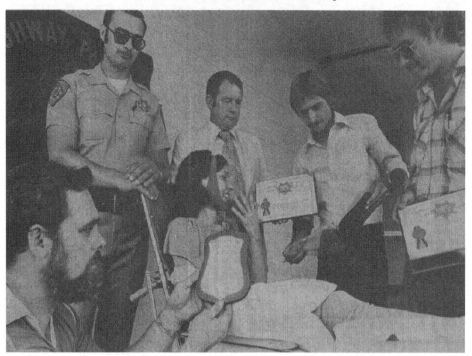

This is a newspaper photo with Pete and Marie Thompson,
she was the Survivor of a 3 fatality accident.

San Diego CHP with new Life Flight Helicopter
Summer 1983

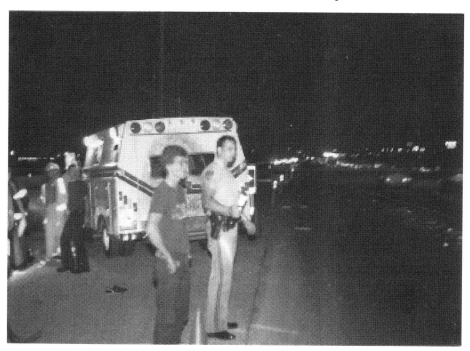

Working another traffic accident scene

Receiving from my Division Chief Ben Killingsworth,
my 2nd Stolen Vehicle Recovery Award (1985)

C. H. P. - Coffee Has Priority

In front of my home with my friend Al Wilkerson

One of CHP's Patrol Vehicles

...on Vacation (1986) San Diego, CA.

Newspaper photo of me working an fatality accident involving
another CHP Officer and Vehicle (1988)

In my Patrol Car (1988)

My retirement party at a restaurant (Feb. 1988)

Ministry

Mission Trip to Mexico (1984)

From a video of me singing at my home church
The Bridge in Bixby, OK. (2013)

BRING A FRIEND  *EVERYONE* IS WELCOME

Full Gospel Business Men's Fellowship International
HIGH SIERRA CHAPTER
INVITES YOU TO OUR
BANQUET MEETING
AT
LITTLE CHARRO'S RESTAURANT
970 NORTH MAIN STREET
BISHOP, CALIFORNIA
SATURDAY EVENING, SEPTEMBER 10, 1988

ED MARR
former Marine "D.I." and California Highway Patrolman

Ed left the Marine Corps after years of serving as a Drill Instructor, "A funny thing happened to him on the way home." He ran into someone who literally changed the course of his life.

A big man at 6' 6", he chose to join the California Highway Patrol. He was unable to begin that position because of a problem dating back several years. Finally after 10 months failure to resolve the problem, "Big Ed" made a deal with Jesus Christ whom he had met the day he left the Marines.

The problem was resolved and Ed has served as "God's man" on the Highway Patrol the past 10 years.

The Lord has worked through him during this time and many have been saved as this uniformed California Highway Patrol Officer came on the scene.

Don't miss this opportunity to hear how God works through the CHP who are committed to Him, bring a friend who doesn't know.

DINNER: $6.00 AT 6:30 P.M. / MEETING AT 7:15 P.M.

TICKETS WILL BE SOLD AT THE DOOR

RESERVATIONS A MUST • CALL BY SEPTEMBER 8, 1988

PLEASE CALL IN CANCELLATIONS
RESERVATIONS ARE ALSO NEEDED FOR SPEAKER AT 7:15.

FOR RESERVATIONS CALL: (619) 873-6464 or 873-8633

This is a flyer from one of the times I have spoken at
Full Gospel Business Men's Fellowship International

C. H. P. - Coffee Has Priority

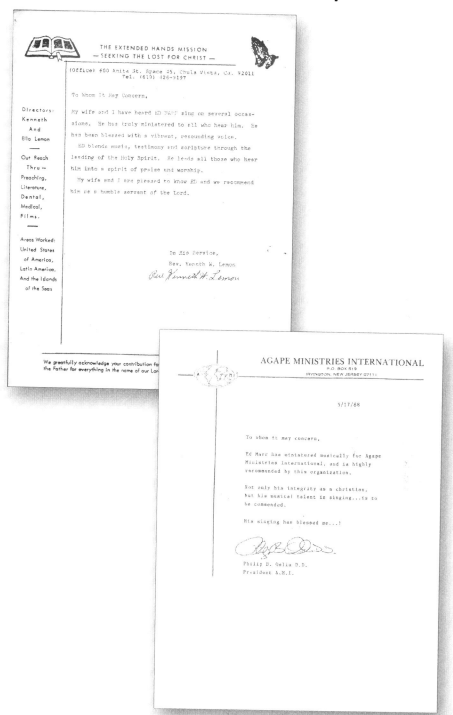

A couple of reference letters from Churches about my Ministry.

Bible School Graduation (1998) with Rev. Bob Nickols
Calvary Cathedral International, Ft. Worth, TX.

Chapter 12
A High Risk Felony Stop for Deuce

"Though I walk in the midst of trouble, thou wilt revive me:
thou shalt stretch forth thy hand against the wrath of mine
enemies, and thy right hand shall save me."
Psalm 138:7

I really don't know why drunk drivers are called deuce. I suppose this expression comes from those who have had one too many. In any event, in the summer of 1983, I worked the south San Diego area on graveyard. Ficky-Wicky had called in sick so this left me as the odd man out for the shift. As it turned out, another officer also called in sick leaving his partner the odd man out as well. So, Officer Chris and I paired up for the evening. From the onset, I sensed that the two of us were not going to get along very well. (This sort of thing happens often between two men, and great care is taken to ensure mutual compatibility between graveyard officers.) Now Chris stood 6'4" though not as heavy as I. His last duty assignment was an area office in the Los Angeles area. Knowing this, I figured that his powers of observation were probably better than mine, based solely on the fact that the Los Angeles area is far busier than life in San Diego.

Early on in our shift and while we were assisting a disabled motorist on the right shoulder of north bound I-5 at "L" street in Chula Vista, a high speed Chevy Camaro passed by northbound and drifting from shoulder to shoulder crossing all four lanes! We immediately took off after the Camaro. I was driving and paced the vehicle at 105 mph. Since I was the senior officer, I instructed Officer Chris of our game plan saying, Look! It is their hands that can kill us. These guys are most likely cho los (a Hispanic gang) and they probably are dirty. So here's what we are going to do. Let's put aside our petty differences and focus on concluding this stop safe and sound, alright Chris? He agreed. I told him, we were going to allow all five passengers out, carefully. You will stand watch over them once they are removed. I said, since it is my out for a deuce, I'll conduct the FSTs (field sobriety tests) in front of the Camaro. In the mean time, you ensure that the passengers remain seated on the ground between our two vehicles and make sure that their hands remain in plain sight at all times. Okay Chris? At this time, I lit up the Camaro and attempted to affect an enforcement stop on the right shoulder of I-5. But since this vehicle was out of control, in that the driver was deuce, it came to a stop on the narrow left shoulder of I-5 over the 24th Street underpass. (Not the best of places to conduct enforcement stops.) The shoulder was barely 7 foot wide. The northbound number one lane was just 18 inches away from the right side of our vehicles. I advised radio dispatch of our location and what all we had. I gave them the vehicle description and license plate prior to stopping. Chris and I exited and approached the Camaro. With weapons drawn, I ordered them to cooperate and for the driver to get out first. I told the driver to sit on the ground and commanded the other occupants to get out keeping their hands in plain sight. Accomplishing this, I directed my attention to the driver and charged Officer Chris to maintain his vigilance.

I took the driver to the front of the Camaro for the FSTs. As I conducted my business with him, I noticed some body movement behind my squad car, silhouetted in the headlights of on coming north bound traffic. It was Chris! He was fighting one of the passengers. Immediately, there appeared over my patrol car a pair of arms and in its hands a scroll. These arms opened the scroll revealing a stick figure sketch of our exact positions!

Seeing this, I intuitively knew that God was with me and I acted upon this supernatural encouragement. I grabbed my driver and shoved him under the front of his Camaro hand cuffed, wedging him there. I then ran passed the other rambunctious passengers, who were all gaining their courage to move against Chris and myself. I grabbed the microphone and called for backup. I took my PR-24 and ran towards Chris and his assailant. I said, Chris, this is the best I can do for you! So I struck the assailant hard on the back of his legs, tripping him. I then spun around on my vertical axis, drawing my revolver at the same time. I turned facing the other passengers who were charging me from behind. I fell to the ground in a seated position, and rolling on my back, I shouted, FREEZE aiming my weapon at them! Three of the four promptly returned to their seat, leaving the largest one who wanted to challenge me. With my weapon drawn and pointed at his chest, I stepped forward, walking him backwards. I said, Return to your seat punk! I said this three times, each time shoving the barrel of my weapon further into his chest. With the third punch, I decked this would be assailant. By the time the other units arrived, the situation had deescalated. As it turns out, each of these bozos had a criminal record and the one assailant against Chris had the longest. We took the driver as deuce and the National City PD took custody of the assailant and his cronies all of which were run up on charges for assault and battery against a peace officer.

On our way back to our beat from the jail, I sensed that Chris was troubled. I asked him what he was thinking. Chris said, Ed, I did what you told me to do. That guy stood up three separate times disregarding my command to remain seated. The third time he stood up, he walked over to me and while standing there in front of me, lit a cigarette and blew the smoke in my face. I commanded him to return to his seat. He responded by burning my left hand with his cigarette. And the fight was on!

Chris went on too say, Ed, I owe you an apology. How's that I asked. Chris said, I've listened to many other officers' comments about you. They told me that you were a stupid man and a lousy officer. Well, tonight having gone through this incident with you, I want you to know that you are not stupid and that you are one of the finest officers I've ever worked with. I never told Chris about God's arms that appeared over top our patrol car.

Chapter 13
Two More Angelic Encounters and a Voice

"Surely thou hast spoken in mine hearing,
and I have heard the voice of thy words, saying,"
Job 33:8

One wet Sunday morning, I was assigned to work the National City area of I-5. During the course of my shift, I received a radio dispatch of a two vehicle collision which occurred in the northbound lanes of I-5 south of Division Street. I was also informed that there was a possible deuce involved. Several minutes later, I arrived and found an occupied wrecked vehicle (V-1) within the northbound number 3 lane. This vehicle sustained heavy front end damage. The female driver was still seated at the wheel. Her passengers (children) had escaped the vehicle prior to my arrival and stood by watching from the right shoulder. As to the other vehicle (V-2) involved, I found it on the left shoulder with heavy rear end damage. Its driver was an elderly woman, who was seated on the center divide guard rail and in the rain. She was visibly shaken up and cold. After securing the collision scene by way of traffic flares, I confronted the female driver inside V-1. I noticed that her skin had been painted gold around her mouth and she had a folded blue, terry cloth rag between her teeth. This rag had been sprayed with gold paint, which indicated to me that this woman (and mother) continued to huff (inhale) the fumes of this paint, even after the impact! I immediately removed her from V-1 and placed her in custody for DUI (Driving Under the Influence). Later, her young children advised me of their mother's addition.

With other units arriving, I was then free to direct my attention to the elderly woman on the guard rail. I spoke with her briefly to ascertain her physical condition. She was really shaken up a bit and very much afraid. As I attempted to comfort her, I felt a tap on my left shoulder from some one standing behind me. I looked back and saw an attractive young woman, who had shoulder length blond hair. I observed her manner of dress. She wore a pink pullover sleeveless sweater, white pleated knee length shorts and sandals. She said, Hello Officer. May I be of some help here? I graciously accepted her assistance. I said to her, Ma'am, you're an angel! And so I asked her to stay with this woman for the time being. I then stood up and turned my back on these two women as I headed back into the traffic lanes. I took 1, 2, 3 steps forward and turned my head to look back at these two women. Now, let me ask you. How much time does it take to walk three steps? Maybe three seconds, right? When I looked back at these two, I saw only the elderly woman! She sat there in the rain with a great big smile on her face, calm as could be! Her glowing countenance was most intriguing to me. Where before hand, she was very disturbed and perhaps disorientated, now her face radiated! I looked around for this other woman, but she was nowhere in sight! Then it hit me! My own words, you're an angel, were rehearsed in my mind! I concluded my task at this collision scene, knowing that Almighty God had my back once again.

On another occasion one evening, I was on routine patrol cruising north on SR-15 from I-5 in the National (Nasty) City area. I was designated the acting Sergeant for the evening shift, so my duties were relatively light in that I had to be free to respond to any scenario that would require my presence or input. In very light traffic, I proceeded north on SR-15. I recall passing a dark colored sedan to my right, that was traveling in the northbound number two lane. I was in the northbound number one lane. Things were quiet, and as my thoughts drifted off on my days off, suddenly there appeared a pair of head lights in front of me! These head lights were traveling south in my lane and were about a half a mile ahead, traveling at freeway speeds and coming straight towards me! Instinctively, I slammed on my brakes in an attempt to duck behind the vehicle to my right. The only problem was that it too slowed abruptly, thereby ruining my chance to save my own bacon! Once again, let me ask you, how long do you think it takes for two vehicles coming towards one another at freeway speeds to close a half mile distance? I'll tell you, it takes only moments!

My patrol unit was not equipped with an overhead light bar. It was equipped with only a ruby red stop light, a siren and wig-wag headlights! I got on the radio and informed radio dispatch of my location and my situation. I told them that if they did not hear from me in five minutes to send help as I had been involved in a head on collision. I no sooner hung up, when I saw this USO (Unidentified Spiritual Object) swoop down out of the darkness and land in front of my stopped vehicle! This angel turned his head towards me and winked. He placed his right hand on the grill plate of my unit and then turned extending his left arm out towards the on coming wrong way vehicle. Immediately this vehicle came to an abrupt stop about 6 or 7 feet from my patrol car! This angel then vanished!

As it turned out, the driver was an elderly man suffering with Alzheimer's and was obviously disorientated. It took a while for me to calm myself down. Have you ever tasted your heart? Let me tell you, it does not taste like chicken! I advised radio dispatch of the situation and requested a tow truck for this vehicle. I determined through the course of my enforcement contact this man's address. I requested dispatch to phone his house. The man's grand-daughter answered. I told dispatch to tell her that I would transport her grandfather home as soon as I could, and to reassure her that he was fine.

The Voice of Words

It was 1345 pm., and my shift had come to a close. On this particular summer afternoon (in 1985) I was about 2 miles from my area office on Pacific Highway which is located about 5 miles or so north of downtown San Diego. I received a dispatch call to respond to Otay Mesa Road east of I-805 to remove an 11-25 (traffic hazard) from the traffic lane. Now, my response time would be at the very least 30 minutes, so I requested dispatch to call on a closer unit, and if this did not work, call the sheriff to see if that agency had a closer unit in the area. By the time radio dispatch contacted me again, I was refueling in anticipation that I would have to respond. You see, although I knew that there were other CHP units closer to this area than I, I also knew that since the shift had concluded, all other officers would not respond in my place. You see, my reputation as a Jesus Freak among the others was tenuous. Consequently, they seldom if ever would do any thing to assist me. Frustrated, I headed for this bogus call whose location was some 25 miles south! I exited I-805 southbound and proceeded east on Otay Mesa Road. Otay Mesa Road at this time was a straight, two lane, east-west roadway within and across the steep hills east of I-805 in south San Diego. As I ascended the steepest hill, I heard a voice saying, there is a westbound yellow sedan accelerating within your eastbound lane attempting to pass seven slower westbound vehicles ahead of it on the opposite side of the crest of this hill. Be ready! Moments later, I met this sedan! It was a yellow 1979 Chevy Monte Carlo and it was accelerating in my east bound lane in an attempt to pass seven westbound vehicles! I turned hard right, leaving the roadway and spun out in the pucker brush. Regaining control of my patrol unit, I accelerated my chariot and gave chase. This bozo never once bothered to pull over after he literally ran me off the road! This inconsideration of his really annoyed me! I caught up with this vehicle, stopping it. I approached the driver on the left side and pinched him a citation for excessive speed and driving left of the double yellow lines. I don't know who was more agitated between us. He was fearful of me and I was so pumped up with adrenalin I had trouble scratching out the citation! Oh by the way, I never found the traffic hazard.

C. H. P. - Coffee Has Priority

Chapter 14
Free Flying Lessons

*"If ye walk in my statutes, and keep my commandments,
and do them… And five of you shall chase an hundred,
and a hundred of you shall put ten thousand to flight:
and your enemies shall fall before you by the sword."
Leviticus 26:3, 8*

Now this particular incident does not contain any spiritual significance as the others, but it is one of my favorite memories. One afternoon about 5 pm, I was on routine patrol on I-5 south bound from I-8 and in heavy commute traffic. I spotted a beat up brown Chevy Pick Up truck traveling south in the number one lane just ahead of me. Its bed was loaded with construction equipment, so I figured that its driver was probably on his way home from a hard day at the building site. I slowly positioned my unit in the south bound number three lane and just off its right rear. From this position, I obtained a good view of the driver. After a few moments, I saw the driver check his mirrors for me. Assuming that I was nowhere around, this driver lifted a bruesky (beer) to his mouth and began to drink. At this time, I pulled forward and flanked his truck from the right. I displayed my colors with the intent that the driver would spot them from the corner of his right eye. Sure enough, it worked. The driver turned his head at my unit forgetting that he held the beer. The beer spilt onto his shirt and he pulled over, for he knew that he had been had! So I made contact with this driver along the left shoulder of I-5 about a mile north of the Front Street exit. He was a little man. He stood 5'4" tall against my 6'6" frame. He was somewhat intoxicated and a bit hostile. After balancing him out,

I informed him to turn around as I was placing him under arrest for DUI. This little man refused to comply. so I reasoned with him saying, Look little man; we can do this anyway you like. But I guarantee you this—I will win and you will loose! Now which will it be? To this he hesitated and sensing his indecision, I said, look, from purely a physical point of view, I have an easy 160 pounds on you. Don't be a fool! So reluctantly, this man surrendered allowing me to cuff him. After hooking his truck, I headed to the county jail where he eventually submitted to a urine test. Now, my prisoner and I were all alone in the jail on the quick release side. This particular room is used extensively by many police agencies for deuce incarcerations. By this I mean that the officers would complete their arrest reports here, while seated with their prisoners prior to leaving the jail facility. Now, this room was probably less than a thousand square feet in floor space. Inside there were three long rows of wooden benches that were permanently attached to the concrete floor and one row of benches attached to the two side walls. The forward facing wall consisted of half concrete below and of plexi-glass above. When I arrived with my prisoner, the passage way in front of the glass was vacant in that the only people in it were the two sheriff deputies. So I instructed my prisoner to sit in the forward corner of this quick release room, while I completed my arrest report.

A few minutes pass, and another CHP Officer arrived with his prisoner. Officer Pete was a new officer to the Patrol and to my area office. He was a nice fellow, but did lack a certain audacity to perform his job as required. (At least this was my assessment.) I glanced at his prisoner and I knew right then I would be in for a fight. This prisoner sported several tattoos and was loud and obnoxious. Officer Pete escorted his prisoner past me to my right, where I sat writing and facing the glass wall and my prisoner. Officer Pete then stopped some 10 feet behind me and uncuffed his prisoner, instructing him to sit down on the wall bench that was to my right. This man complied, but as soon as Officer Pete turned his back, his prisoner stood up in defiance, shouting. This man told Officer Pete in no uncertain terms to go to hell and that Pete would have to force him to sit! Officer Pete attempted to reason with his arrest, but without benefit. This man continued to mouth off all kinds of vulgarities at Officer Pete, stating in essence that he knew martial arts and that he was going to kick Officer Pete's butt, to put it mildly! This man gained the psychological advantage over Officer Pete and he knew it! Now, it is customary that the arresting officer maintain control of his prisoner at all times. This also pertains to the psychological advantage as well, and that at no time should another officer interfere without a request to do so. This helps to ensure the credibility of the officer and for the arrest report as well. However, Officer Pete was genuinely intimidated by his prisoner. Knowing this, the prisoner paraded around in the quick release room, where I was trying to complete my report! During all of this, I never once looked up at this prisoner. I did not have to, for I knew the lay of the floor plan and I could see his feet and legs as well as hear his voice and the direction from which he spoke. Sheepishly, Officer Pete begged his prisoner to return to his seat. Again and again, Officer Pete pleaded! By this time, I was getting annoyed. From my seated position and without lifting my head, I stated out loud, Look slick! I know that this fine young Officer has instructed you many times to return to your seat. He's even begged you! Now, I am not going to beg you, but I will tell you only once to return to your seat. If you don't, then I will plant you there! Do you understand slick? To this, Officer Pete's prisoner walked over to me and stood to my left. From my seated position, he shouted, @#$%! I'll kick your $%^&. As he said this to me, I watched his hands double up into fists. Since he was within my personal airspace, I considered him to be a threat to me personally, so I calmly placed my pencil down and as I stood to my feet, I grabbed this punk by his shirt and threw him up and over. He struck the wall to my right about 9 feet above the floor horizontally! At this point, gravity took over and he slid down the wall like slime and landed on his back on the bench below. Upon making contact with the bench, we all heard a loud crack! This man laid there face up on the bench in sever pain saying, awh, awh, awh! You s.o.b., you broke my back! I can't move! When I turned to the sheriff deputy in the hall to call for help, I noticed a bus load of other prisoners facing me spread eagle against the glass. Their eyes and mouths were wide open! The deputy called for help alright. He requested immediate assistance to prevent a potential prisoner riot!

Meanwhile, Officer Pete stood speechless. I told him, Pete! Let this be a lesson to you! You must maintain control of your prisoners at all costs! Then my prisoner stated to me, Officer Marr. I want to apologize to you for my behavior out on the road and I thank you for not doing that to me! I told him to shut up! I requested the deputy to call the ambulance for this injured man. I spoke with Officer Pete and told him how he should write his report and that I would write a supplemental to it. I then called my shift supervisor and informed him of the situation. Meanwhile, as we waited for the ambulance, Pete's prisoner stated to me, Officer! I've had many a run in with law enforcement in times past, but I've never! Man, you don't know your own strength! His remarks reminded of Marine Charles L. from the streets of Chicago.

The ambulance arrived and the paramedics took him to the county hospital, where Officer Pete and I met our shift supervisor. Our supervisor was genuinely concerned for my job, in that word could get out about this and I could be charged with excessive force. Apparently, this prisoner was aware of our concern and he asked my supervisor and me to approach his hospital bed. So we did. The prisoner said to the supervisor. Sergeant!

This officer did nothing wrong. I slipped and fell on some water at the jail! My supervisor then said, do you mean to tell me that you were clumsy and you injured yourself? The prisoner said, yes sir! That is exactly what I am telling you. The supervisor was satisfied and very much relieved. He said to Officer Pete and me, just complete your reports and Marr, I want to see you at the office afterwards, okay? After this prisoner said what he did to us, I felt lousy, for injuring him. I wanted to let the man go and by him a great big steak! I concluded my contact with the man shaking his hand, thanking him for his consideration and his integrity. In departing, I told him, Oh by the way! Remember this. It only hurts when you laugh!

Chapter 15
Pauline Bunyan

"Herein is love, not that we loved God, but that he loved us [first], and sent his son to be the propitiation for our sins."
1 John 4:10

One Sunday morning in the summer of 1984, I received a dispatch call to respond to the Coronado Bay Bridge to assist the San Diego P.D. with a suicidal woman. I responded from the southern most part of my beat, so it took me some 10 minutes to arrive running code. As I approached the bridge from the south on I-5 northbound, I recalled thinking of its overall dimensions. The bridge is 1.6 miles in length and at mid span the bridge is 360 feet above the San Diego Bay, and it takes a paint crew 18 plus years to strip and recoat the bridge with fresh paint from one end to the other. I thought of the 2 times I walked the cat walk underneath the super structure and how fearful I was looking down at the water through the grated mesh.

I thought of the many other suicides that I have been personally involved with, some of which did in fact jump to their death. I recall timing the descent of several stones of varying sizes, which I dropped from mid span a few months earlier just to determine the length of time between the span and the impact with the water. Consistently, each stone took 11 seconds. Through some calculus computations, it was determined that any object hitting the water would do so at a respectable speed of 87 mph!

When I finally did arrive on the bridge mid span, I certainly did not expect to see any physical altercation, but to my amusement, I did and the woman was winning! I remained seated in my patrol unit, enjoying the humor of this battle! Here she was, standing every bit of 6'4" tall. She must have weighed in at 240 pounds easy! She had long, flaming red hair. She wore a black / red checkered Pendleton style shirt/jacket, faded blue jeans and tan work boots. In short she was one of the largest and strongest women I've ever seen, and by this I mean height to weight ratio and proportions!

So here we were mid span in the midst of a center switch lane, with two traffic lanes in each direction and no shoulder. There were six SDPD officers attempting to subdue this monster of a gal (a.k.a.: Pauline Bunyan), but they were sorely loosing the battle. I saw flashlights and batons flying through the air! I saw one to three officers flying into the air and the roar this woman made would rival any wounded lion! She reminded me of a young Merlyn Oslen in the John Wayne movie, The Undefeated! Several of the officers had torn uniforms and skinned elbows and knee caps. It was hilarious, at least from my spectator position. This was as good as any WWF wrestling match!

Now, these officers were aware of my presence and they strongly encouraged me to join in. I basically informed them that the CHP does not pay me enough to fight with the public, especially when it is not my fight! After awhile, Pauline Bunyan tired down and the officers were able to subdue her at which time they removed her from the bridge. I informed the SDPD that I would transport this woman to County Mental Health (CMH) for them, if they would kindly inventory her vehicle, which she had parked in the center switch lane, mid span. They accepted my gracious proposition and I followed behind as we all drove to the parking lot at the bridge toll plaza on the Coronado Island side of the bridge. Winded and bleeding, the officers gladly surrendered Pauline over to me. At which time I cuffed her and seated her in the right front seat of my chariot. All this time, Pauline snarled and hollered, rocking my unit side to side with her mighty attempts to break free of the cuffs and the seat belt. Truly, I knew that I most certainly had my hands full with this behemoth!

I finally cleared from the bridge and proceeded to CMH. I could not hear myself think and certainly could not hear my radio, with her outcries and emotional out bursts! So, I told radio dispatch that I would contact them once I arrived at the hospital, but until then keep me monitored. While still on the bridge, I heard the Spirit of God say in my ear, Ed, Tell her that you love her! I replied, Lord, You have got to be kidding, right? Again, I hear, tell her that you love her! With much reluctance, I whimpered and said to Pauline, I love ya. It did not make a dent, so I said to my Father, See! It did not work! It didn't even faze her! Again, the Lord spoke to me and this time with some degree of consternation, He said, Tell her you Love Her! So once again, I turned to earsplitting Pauline Bunyan and said awkwardly, I love you! but it had no affect, just as before. Raising my voice, I again said, I love you! This time Pauline Bunyan stopped her clamor and looked at me, apparently shocked that a law enforcement officer would even say this. She then continued on with her high-pitched grating cries of deep pain and personal anguish. I then bellowed out to her, LADY, I said, I LOVE YOU! This time I got her attention and she looked at me and stated, How can you a *&^%$ pig, love someone like me? I replied, honestly lady. You're absolutely right. In and of myself, I could never love someone like you. But I do know someone who does love you just as you are! All you have to do is receive His love. Are you willing to listen to me?

For the duration of our trip to the hospital, I spoke of God's love for me personally, for humanity and particularly for her. She became somberly attentive. I testified to her about several of my Unidentified Spiritual Encounters (USEs) and how often Almighty God had saved my life. This conversation lasted until we arrived at the hospital. I notified radio dispatch of my arrival and that things were code four. I escorted Pauline Bunyan inside for observation and admission, where we waited several minutes. I had Pauline take a seat. While inside, Pauline asked me to pray for her. I told her that I would do more than that. So I got on my knees taking her hands in mine. I then prayed over her and with her, leading her in a prayer of salvation. She wept bitterly as the convicting power of the Spirit called Holy swept upon her and within her. She was now born again! Together we stood up and in cleansing tears of joy; she gave me one of the biggest hugs ever! She literally picked me up off the floor and this was no easy accomplishment for most, since I weighed 275 pounds.

Departing the hospital, I headed straight for my home church. I knew that services would be in progress, but I had just experienced one of the most powerful events of salvation that I just had to tell somebody, lest I explode! Pastor Dwaine Lee was already well into his message when I arrived. I spoke with an usher giving him a note indicating my desire to testify now. He walked up to my Pastor and gave him the note. Pastor Lee graciously called me forward and allowed me to testify to some 1200 people on that Sunday morning of the wonderful manner in which the power of God's love can overcome adversities in one's life. Truly, this experience in my opinion is one for the books!

By contrast, late one night, Officer Vick and I were notified, by a passing motorist, of an adult white male sitting on the south bridge rail of the Coronado Bay Bridge. It was just past 2 am. Having arrived mid span, Vick parked the patrol car in the center switch lane in the immediate vicinity of this distraught man. We both exited and positioned ourselves several feet on either side away from this potential jumper. With open arms and adjuring voices, both Vick and I attempted to help this man. However, as we spoke and closed in ever so carefully, this man rose from the rail and looked at me. His countenance resembled one who has a predetermination for death. This man stepped away from me and walked towards Vick. He then he leaped over the side! Vick and I ran over to the side and waited for the sound of impact into the water. We heard it, eleven seconds later. Vick and I turned towards each other scolding each other! After the initial affect of this jump wore off, both of us realized that the reason we became so upset towards one another was because this man deprived us of doing our very best to save his life! Aside from this reality, I stated to Vick, I now know what it means and feels like to be my brother's keeper. Vick asked, what do you mean, Ed? I said, it is one thing to take someone's life for self-defense and it is another thing to work a fatality, and it is still another thing to be involved in a murder case. Vick, all these are tragic enough, but to watch someone take their own life and that unnecessarily has its own particular heartache. Vick simply said, I know what you mean. So we notified dispatch of this suicide and requested the assistance from the Harbor Patrol. Several minutes later, the Harbor Patrol appeared and removed the body from the water. It was at this time that Vick and I learned that this man was stationed at the 32nd Street Naval Station. On the patrol boat and having obtained the identification, the Harbor Patrol told us that this man had been removed from the bridge two nights earlier. In other words, this man had either contemplated jumping then or attempted to jump but failed. Vick and I then notified his command, and that sure was tough duty.

Chapter 16
The Pursuit and the Shell Game

"But ye said, No; for we will flee upon horses;
therefore shall ye flee: and, We will ride upon the swift;
therefore shall they that pursue be swift."
Isaiah 30:16

So here it was spring of 1985 and to my surprise Lt. Joe was now second in command in the San Diego area office, whether I liked it or not! During the course of his little vocalizations, he seemed to look for me and when he spotted me, he held his stare at me! This caused me alarm, for I sensed that this man would eventually spell trouble. Well, time went on and all of us officers had to adjust our routine to accommodate the new restrictions and mandates that filtered down from our new illustrious supervisors, and let me tell you, we were not happy campers! However, there were a select few amongst our ranks, who seemed to gravitate towards these new mandates. Most of us sort of expected this to occur, and being true to form, three to five officers whom we all identified as potential brown noses did not let us down.

Now, time went on, and I spent the majority of my career working the South Bay area of San Diego County. This included the Port of Entry at San Ysidro as well. Many times, I would be on reports either at the Port of Entry hooking a deuce or some other offender or already at the jail. Consequently, I had very little time for patrol. Month after month, my daily activity chart was left blank so far as writing citations went; but my arrest tally was way up there. Well, this inactivity seemed to be the very thing that my supervisors needed to use against me. Week after week, and month after month, my immediate shift supervisor leaned on me to bring up my citation counts. I argued that it was impossible, since I have been swamped with arrest reports and other criminal investigations. Soon, other supervisors began to lean on me for the same thing. Previously, my work ethic was applauded; now it was ridiculed! Then in August of 1986, I had to work an extended work week, another eleven day stretch. I was very tired. Although I had just two days off, I knew that this time off would not fully recharge my batteries for the job. On Saturday, the 23rd of August, I reluctantly returned for work. I had just purchased a new residence and I had spent my two days off landscaping my property. So I was physically fatigued by late that morning. My wife suggested that I call in, but my integrity or pride would not allow me to do that. I thought, well, perhaps this shift would be a quiet one and that if things did go haywire, I would just pace myself and allow the other officers to take up my slack. By this time and because of our new Captain and his hatchet man (Lt. Joe), many officers had already transferred out of area, as our office acquired the bad reputation, throughout the state, as being the least desirable office to work in. Consequently, there were very few new transferees coming in. This meant that for me and the few officers who resided in town, we had to pull double even triple duty!

The shift was going very well for me. Things were slow and that was just fine. I recall nodding off at the wheel from time to time, because it was so quiet. At approximately 1830 hours, I decided to head home for chow. I traveled south bound on I-805 and in the National City area, when I spotted another CHP officer, from my office, on a routine traffic stop in the center divide just south of the 43rd Street overpass. I decided to pull over and say howdy for a brief few. I then took off again and as I approached the "H" Street exit ramp in Chula Vista, this officer informed me (car to car) of a very high speed, red colored café style (rice burner) motorcycle traveling south on I-805 at least 100 mph plus coming up behind me. He said that the rider was wearing a full face, red helmet that sported a broad dark blue horizontal racing stripe around the temple areas of the helmet. He was described to me as wearing a loose fitting long sleeve blue denim jacket and blue Levi trousers. I acknowledged his transmission and promptly exited at "H" Street. I waited on the on-ramp and monitored south bound I-805 for seemingly five minutes or so. At the estimated speed of this motorcycle, which the officer told me, I figured that it should have already passed my location. But since it did not and I was hungry, I proceeded down the ramp and headed for home and hopefully a nice meal. Just as I entered the acceleration lane in traffic, I spotted the motorcycle. It was traveling south in the number one lane and located directly across from me four lanes to my left. I confirmed the description of the rider, that it was the same as told me. This motorcyclist attempted to blend in with surrounding traffic in an attempt to avoid detection from us smokies, for he obviously saw the other officer further back and no matter how fast his bike was, the rider knew that he could not out run the radio.

So I carefully repositioned my chariot about 100 feet behind the motorcycle in the number one south bound lane. I wanted to obtain the license plate number, but I could not read the small print. I initially paced him at 65 mph. and I accelerated to close the gap. I figured, I would just give the rider a stiff warning and let it go at that. As I closed in on him, I lit him up and tapped my Public Address System to get his attention. The rider hesitated and glanced back at me through his mirrors. And the pursuit was on! Fortunately, traffic grew lighter the further south we went. My chariots' top speed was 135 and that with a strong tail wind and a steep down hill run! This rider out distanced me by at least a ½ mile in no time at all. I figured this was a waste of time so I shut it down. After all, I wanted to eat. To my surprise, the motorcycle slowed down considerably and waited for me to catch up! Since we both were headed in the same direction, I again accommodated him with a chase. I was hoping that his vehicle would blow a piston or perhaps tumble in the freeway. I had hoped for this, so as to take one more Slick Willy from the road. But this was not to be. Again the motorcycle pulled way ahead of me, so I discontinued the pursuit. Again, the rider slowed down and waited for me to catch up. (There's an adage that says, fool me once, shame on you. Fool me twice, shame on me.) Because of the distance between us, this rider apparently lost sight of me. So he presumably surmised that I had discontinued the pursuit altogether. As it turned out, I saw this motorcycle exit at Main Street, which happened to be my exit. Now, this ramp is a steep descending exit, which is 3/10 of a mile long. At its south end, this ramp terminates at the northbound prolongation line to east-west Main Street.

So I exited I-805 and my speed was slowing from 135 mph. I managed to slow enough to negotiate the turn behind the motorcycle, whose rider I did surprise. Mind you, the closest I ever got to this bike was when I initially lit it up. Knowing the lay of the land and what the road conditions were like, I fully expected to catch up with this crotch rocket on Main Street in traffic at the nearest controlled intersection about a quarter mile west of I-805. However, the rider blew the intersection accelerating all the more! I too blew the intersection, but only after I cleared it for cross traffic. The last glimpse of this motorcycle I had was just before I cleared this intersection. It was here that I saw it climb the hill about another quarter mile ahead. When I cleared the intersection, I looked forward and saw the motorcycle traveling slowly as it went up the hill. I figured that this guy wanted to continue to play games, so once again I took off after him. He allowed me to close the distance. I pulled up along side him, to his right. It appeared to be the same bike I had been chasing and that the rider was in fact wearing a red full face helmet with that broad racing stripe at the temples, as well as a loose fitting dark blue denim jacket and denim trousers. It all seemed to match. I figured this was my man. However, as I was confirming his description and that of the bike, I inadvertently allowed my vehicle to drift towards the left into the motorcycle. We collided at a slow speed on west bound Main Street about a half mile east of Broadway. I stopped immediately and requested my supervisor. I then helped the rider to his feet and breached him over the hood of my unit and cuffed him. He was bewildered that I had arrested him! He assured me that he saw a high speed motorcycle traveling west on Main street just as he made his left turn onto Main Street from a private drive just west of the first controlled intersection. Soon, other citizens informed me of the very same thing. I soon realized that I had been suckered! It was as though someone had played a shell game with me and I lost. As soon as this reality set in, I heard in my ear, Son, this is that which I spoke of! As it turned out, this motorcyclist with me was operating without a driver's license and in control of a bike, whose license plates had been switched! I promptly arrested this man for the observed violations and waited for my shift supervisor and other CHP units to assist.

Chapter 17
Are You One of Those Christians?

"And then shall many be offended, and shall betray one another, and shall hate one another."
Matthew 24:10

In a previous chapter, I had mentioned that I heard the audible voice of God speak to me at 28,000 feet on my flight to Sacramento, California. He said, You will not go a full twenty years towards a full CHP retirement, but know this, that something will happen to you in the later half of the decade of the eighties that will separate you from your employment with the CHP! I never forgot this and in the spring of 1985 there was a change of command at the San Diego area office. Specifically, we lost our beloved old school Captain and his lieutenant (second in command). In their place, the officers of the San Diego area were all introduced to our (new school) Captain and another Lieutenant whom I shall identify as Joe, and suffice it to say that these men were of a different breed.

I met these men during an afternoon briefing, prior to hitting the road. All of us officers listened to their short impersonal monologue with our usual inattentiveness. As they spoke, I heard the Holy Ghost whisper in my ear; these are they of whom I have told you of. Watch them! I knew intuitively what He meant. You see, it was in the fall of 1982 that I had a desire to get off the road for a while. I had already applied for the special duty position known as Back Ground Investigator. During the process of selection, all candidates for this position where required to sit before a panel of uniformed judges. The panel I sat before consisted of one sergeant and two other division officers. All three had the task of screening all applicants for the best candidate. The sergeant at that time was the same man (Joe) who now stood before me as this lieutenant in this briefing.

I recall when I sat before this panel. I wore a nice dark blue suit and attached to the lapel of my suit coat I had a bronze colored metal TBN stick pin. Now, I knew the other two officers on this panel and they were very much aware of my work ethic. I felt very confident that I would be in strong contention for this position. But during the course of my interview, the Sergeant (Joe) whom I met for the very first time was curious about my stick pin. He asked me, Officer Marr, are you one of those Christians? I stated that I was, and then asked him why he asked. Noticing my stick pin, he asked what it was and what it represented. So I told him that had I obtained it several months earlier from the TBN headquarters in Tustin, California when I was there on a tour of the facility. He didn't say another word about it other than document my statement on his note pad. In time, I would learn that I was overlooked for the Back Ground Investigator position because of Sergeant Joe's disparaging remarks about me, in spite of the wonderful recommendations my area office supervisors gave me.

The Article

It was the Christmas Season of 1986. Officer Al Wilkerson, my good friend and brother in Christ, thought it a noble deed to write a simple Christmas invitation to the officers of the San Diego area office in hopes that all or some would accept Jesus Christ as their personal Lord and Savior. He displayed this little invitation on the grease board in the men's locker room, and you should know that whatever is placed upon this board would be subject to all manner of ridicule! Through the years, I have seen many off color jokes and other foolish commentary written on this board, and so I knew that Al's gracious invitation would be treated no differently. Three weeks passed by when Al met me at the office for our shift. We suited up for our shift, and walked past this board. He stopped me and basically said, Ed, Just look at all this! Have you read any of this? I said, I preferred not to, however since Al brought it all to my attention, I did read most of it. I was somewhat irritated by all this satire. I could not wait to hit the local watering hole! My mind had been ignited with divine outrage! At the Days Inn, I sat alone and wrote out a full page commentary of my own and in this article, I addressed the overall mind set of these ungodly and blasphemous statements made toward Al's simple, unobtrusive invitation. Although I don't recall all that I had written, I do recall the following:

To the Officers of the San Diego Area Office,

I find it amazing that the Word of God does not have equal consideration in this office and within your hearts along with all your pornography, profanity and vulgarities! Even the women in the front office possess color photographs of naked men in the compartments of their desks, and yet the Word of God is given nothing! As far as I am concerned, every one of you who have made these comments to Officer Al Wilkerson's invitation is a poisonous viper! All of you come from a nest of venomous snakes; so go ahead, write your pitiful remarks about this article! And when you do, know this, that you are proving my point!

After the office had closed for business, I returned to the office and posted my article and then left. At the end of my shift and again when I returned the next day for work, I saw several officers huddled together reading my article! Not a single comment was ever made against it. However, the next day, Al observed the Captain and Lt. Joe reading the article. Al indicated that both became very irate, and that Lt. Joe's countenance had changed! He removed the article and took it to his office. That was the last time it was ever seen, and this occurred during the second week of December, 1986.

Kara Knot

As usual I was working the second shift in the south end. One evening, I was refueling my chariot at the gas pump in the back lot of my area office. I arrived a bit early, as I had some reports to complete. As I refueled, Officer Craig drove up to the pumps on the opposite side. He stepped out and I noticed scratches on his face. I did not think much of it, but I did ask him how he obtained those scratches. He in essence told me that he fell against the fence having slipped on some spilt fuel at the pumps earlier in the evening. I accepted his explanation, for I knew that he was the hottest pencil in the office, which means he drove an average 300 miles per shift. The date was December 29th, 1986.

Now, the second shift consisted of fourteen officers in all and we were assembled in the briefing room the next day (the 30th), when Sergeant Dick (our shift supervisor) gave us a B.O.L. (Be on the Look Out) for a white Volkswagen Bug, which was driven by a young woman named, Kara Knot. Apparently, she did not return home as expected the night before so her parents issued a missing persons report to all police agencies. Sergeant Dick cautioned the officers working the north end of San Diego County, since this was where Kara resided.

The following day, I assembled in the briefing room again and along with the rest of my shift officers prior to hitting the road. Once again, Sergeant Dick addressed us and stated that the white VW had been found on an abandoned frontage road off the Mercy Road exit on I-805 on the north end, and that Kara's body had been located! He went on to say that her body was found in a dried up creek bed beneath an old bridge some distance from the location of the VW bug. Now, Officer Craig was seated directly behind me and Officer Al Wilkerson. Upon hearing this, Officer Craig stood up and stated, Sure! That's the perfect place to commit murder! If I were the murderer that is precisely where I would kill her! Immediately, all of us pointed at Officer Craig and in unison stated lightheartedly, here's her killer! Here's her killer! However, both Al and I felt a chill travel up our spine, when Officer Craig spoke as he did.

Two nights later, while I was at home enjoying a night off, the office called me and ordered me to come in. I asked what was going on. The officer told me that I would find out soon enough and that all officers were being called in. Upon my arrival, I found the briefing room packed out. After we all assembled together, the area Captain and Lt. Joe along with all seven area sergeants entered the room. Instantly, all of us officers sensed that something big was about to be unloaded on us. The Captain spoke and informed us that Officer Craig had been arrested for the murder of Kara Knot.

The Inquisition

Well, getting back to my infamous motorcycle pursuit, I was grilled for hours on the following Monday morning, the 25th of August. I admitted that I had made an error in judgment and I acknowledged that the collision was my fault, but that was not sufficient for these area supervisors. Suddenly I found myself sitting before an inquisition! It was certainly overkill, at least from my perspective. I was asked several structural questions, such as what the gradient of I-805 was as well as that of the Main Street off ramp! I was asked to provide specific structural details of the roadway itself! I thought, surely, they knew that I am not a structural engineer! Hours went by. Ficky-Wicky was by my side, as he was the area office Officers' Representative in all matters pertaining to officer mishaps, such as mine. His duty was to assist me in answering specific questions, which could be deemed incriminating. However, Lt. Joe, who presided over this inquisition demanded that Ficky-Wicky keep silent and that since He considered this incident a serious breach of professionalism, I had to answer all questions, regardless. To this command, Ficky-Wicky whimpered away and I was left to answer for my actions alone.

I was threatened with prison time on charges of attempted manslaughter! Sergeant Dick told me, Officer Marr! I am your adversary and you must remember to conduct yourself in that light! Do you understand? Right then I knew that I was in for a prolonged ordeal, given the overall tenor of this inquisition and the other interrogations that followed. Nineteen months would pass, and during this season of supervisory harassment, I was ordered to outline all the Departmental General Orders as well as the Physical Methods of Arrest policies. I submitted several outlines, and did so in a punctual manner. Every outline was written in a neat, concise fashion. I even included a cover letter, which expressed my sincere gratitude to my supervisors for their interests in my career improvement! But in spite of my very best efforts to comply with all orders, it seemed that it was not enough.

Seven different supervisors were ordered to pressure me heavily, whenever I was in uniform. In fact, every time Sgt. Dick had the day off, certain supervisors would place on his desk stacks of documents which claimed that I had misbehaved during his absence, and upon his return to duty, he would be overwhelmed in amazement of these written accusations! My only explanation to Sgt. Dick was that these papers had been planted. Although I could not prove this, I knew intuitively that by order of the Captain and Lt. Joe, other area office supervisors were probably all threatened with disciplinary action if they refused! (This would be eventually revealed to me, after the fact.) Never mind the fact that I had been the area office primary Self-Defense Safety Instructor for the previous five years! Never mind the fact that I was a FTO (Field Training Officer) and on several occasions, served as an acting sergeant! Forget all about the commendations that I had received from outside sources for my exemplary work ethic as well as being a seasoned road warrior! Let's forget about these and center our focus upon politics and down right meanness! Talk about unethical conduct and behavior within the rank and file of leadership! I would never wish what I went through on my worst enemy! The stress of it all caused me to lose weight. My marriage was strained to the breaking point, and my morale plummeted so much so that I regretted going to work. Although I never despised the uniform, I most certainly learned to loathe the harassment of leadership.

Chapter 18
The Harassment Continues

"They were stoned, they were sawn asunder, were tempted, were slain with the sword; they wandered about in sheepskins and goatskins; being destitute, afflicted, tormented: (Of whom the world was not worthy :) they wandered in deserts, and in mountains, and in dens, and caves of the earth."
Hebrews 11:37, 38

Prior to all this however, I had been approached by several sergeants for counseling. Time after time, it was the same old refrain! Marr, my name is ------------------! It is not sergeant! Why can't you consider your supervisors as your friends? Again and again, I would have to explain my reasons for such formality. I stated, Sergeant, I am aware of your interests in me personally, but your interest is limited to my job performance only and not to my social activities outside the job. I said, that as supervisors it would be your duty to discipline me or any other officer should the need arise. But the real issue that most officers had with me was the fact that I did not participate in their revelry! I would attend their choir practice from time to time, but I always retained my integrity so far as my sobriety and my senses went.

Many times, individual officers would sit with me in private and question my maturity as well as my super spiritual disposition. Often I was told, Marr, you wear the same uniform as the rest of us. You perform your duties better than most of us, and yet some how you are different. Sure, a profane word slips from time to time, but that just proves that you are human. But essentially, you don't smoke, you don't cuss, you don't play the field and you don't drink! Why is that, Marr? At times, I've had sergeants take me off to the side and accuse me of being a rogue cop and that I enforced my own brand of law enforcement! On these discussions, I would ask, Sergeant! Do I have any complaints from the motoring public? Of course their only response had to be No, since I had none!

Through the heat of this supervisory harassment, I was even approached one time by a friend, Officer Lynn. He hailed from the state of Virginia, so he and I had something in common since we both had resided back east. He stated, Ed, I think you know that I am your friend and as your friend, I feel I must tell you something that no doubt will offend you. Ed, I know that you are a religious man. I wish all of us were as you, but the fact of the matter is; there is no room for Jesus Christ in law enforcement! He was right about one thing, his words cut straight to my heart! Holding back tears, we each went our separate ways. Through the course of my shift, I wept, rehearsing his words over and over. I knew that my heartache was just a smidgeon of how Almighty God is pained in His heart over the unsuppressed carnality of all impenitent men!

Completing my shift, I tried to enjoy the next two days off, but I could not free my mind from Officer Lynn's comments. So I spent my days off weeping, asking God to give me something to say in reply. On my first work day back, I approached Officer Lynn in the back lot of our area office and said, Lynn my friend, do you recall those harsh, but truthful words which you stated to me a few days ago? He said that he did. I asked him if he really meant what he said. He indicated that he did. So in response, I said to him, Lynn, I want to thank you for your honesty, but what I think you meant to say but did not have the courage to say is this. It is not a matter that Jesus Christ is not welcomed in law enforcement. The real issue is that you won't welcome Jesus Christ in your own heart! Upon hearing this, Lynn turned beat red and flaming mad! I said, Lynn my friend, you have a good day! So I turned and walked away, leaving him standing in his rage.

Occasionally, an officer suggested to me that I should get all tanked up on booze and leap from the mid span of the Coronado Bay Bridge! At such times, I would ask why they would make such a statement to me. Their reply was, Hell! If I was going through what all the supervisors are putting you through, I couldn't handle it! I would either put a bullet in my skull or commit suicide just to free myself from the misery! These rare comments were very insightful for me, because it confirmed the collective ulterior motive of all my supervisors. Namely, they were pushing me to do something really foolish while on the job, such as kill somebody, which would only justify their true heart intentions or they were pushing me with such intensity in hopes that I would kill myself! Either way, their efforts would have been warranted, at least in their mind!

The Last Day

For nineteen months, I did endure this continuous gauntlet! I spent many days parked in my chariot, crying my guts out! All officers, except for Al Wilkerson, avoided me like the plague! I was the brunt of every joke and condescending remark! I very seldom received calls. Either Almighty God saw to that Himself, or the orders were given to radio dispatch to pass me by, preferring another officer to me. On February 8, 1988, I was at work and just commencing my shift when I had reason to speak with a sergeant in his office. I saw Sergeant Tim typing at his desk. He saw me, and asked me a question for his report. I asked him why he needed such personal information and he told me that he was typing out another reprimand and that I could expect to be called in later to receive it. By this time, I had become impervious to the supervisory intimidations and other antics. I thought nothing more of it and after our briefing concluded, I walked out to my patrol vehicle. Suddenly I was approached by Officer Sparky. Sparky told me, Ed, Lt. Joe has ordered the sergeants to initiate termination papers against you! Now get yourself in there and fight for your rights! You have to consider your career, your family and your future! I told Sparky, I just left the Sergeant's office. I saw Sgt. Tim typing another reprimand. At least that is what he told me. Sparky then said, Ed, he lied to you! Right now, Sgt. Tim is preparing a termination package on you! Ed, if you don't stand up for yourself, you will lose your employment and your pension! I said, Sparky you are mistaken! Sgt. Tim told me directly that he was typing up another reprimand. Sparky simply stated, Ed, they are all lying to you! But it is your life! Upon hearing this news, I suddenly felt very strange within. I became very anxious and sickened. It seemed that all the months of harassment finally caught up with me in a moment! I walked back into the office, and headed straight for the sergeant's office. I knocked and Sergeant Dick opened the door. I looked inside and noticed that Lt. Joe was there, along with four other sergeants. I stated, Sergeant Dick, I am not capable of performing my duties today in a professional manner. I request a sick day! Sergeant Dick stood there smiling ear to ear and said, Marr, tell me how do you feel? I repeated myself and added, I feel very awkward inside. I have the shakes. He then said, yea, but how do you really feel, Marr? Sergeant I just told you. He said, I heard you, but how do you really feel? Sensing that he wanted me to express myself in a very personal manner, I said, how do I really feel? Are you asking me what my state of mind is? I'll tell you Sergeant Dick! I feel like I want to go out back to the pull up bar and crank out three sets of thirty! I feel like punching some holes in the wall! How do I really feel, Sergeant Dick? I see six supervisors in this office. I feel like ripping into each and every one of you either together or individually! As I stood there at the door, I started to disrobe. I said, yes, that is exactly how I feel. I want to rip your hearts out and stomp on them and then shove them back inside between your cheeks, and I don't mean those on your face! What's more, I won't need my gun belt and I certainly won't need my revolver! As I took off my shirt, I said, all I'll need are my own two howitzers right here! I stepped into the office, pushing Sergeant Dick aside and walked towards my adversaries. Immediately Lt. Joe climbed into a metal closet and closed the door. He stuck his hand out and said in a high pitched voice; get that man out of here! Sergeant Dick called for Officer Al Wilkerson to return to the office. I changed clothes and waited for his arrival. In the meantime, I was instructed to speak with Lt. Joe in his office. I told Sergeant Dick, I don't trust any of you people and especially Lt. Joe! I said, besides, Lt. Joe will have our conversation recorded and I don't need another bout like that! Sergeant Dick related that Lt. Joe had already informed him that whatever is said in his office would be on the QT! Reluctantly, I did accompany Sergeant Dick. Lt. Joe ordered me to take a seat. I refused to do so. I was in such a state of mind, that I could not tell you what all Lt. Joe said. But I do know this. As he spoke to me, I asked him if he was recording our conversation. Lt. Joe told me that he was not taping. As he spoke, I noticed a flickering green light inside the slightly opened top desk drawer in his office. He no sooner denied the recording, when I swiftly opened that desk drawer and exposed the operating tape recorder! Catching him in a bold face lie, I simply stated, you bastard, end of conversation, and walked out. I retreated to the back fence line of the parking lot, where I lifted my hands in praise to Almighty God, making no bones about my love for Him, and I did not care who or how many supervisors saw me! I remained at the fence line until Al Wilkerson arrived. In short order, I hopped into his unit and was taken to the Medical Industrial Office for observation.

I was in tears and yet I recall a sense of power and strength like I have never known! My good friend Al wept along with me and I thanked him for his friendship through it all. I told him that this would be my last day in uniform. Al then said, Ed, do you remember what you told me several years ago about what Almighty God told you would happen to you in the later half of the decade of the eighties? I had forgotten this, but when Al brought it up, I could not help but know that this was all by design and by God's intention for my life! In spite of Lt. Joe's best efforts to deny me, I was successful in acquiring my disability pension, although this entire tribulation left its mark on my psyche. By this I mean that I experienced a post CHP stress syndrome which stayed with me up until I left California for Texas. Although I no longer was to wear the uniform, I could not deny the fact that law enforcement got into my blood, even to this very day!

For the next year, I had to keep medical appointments. I visited five different psycho-analysts, and was required to complete a series of examinations with each doctor. I was asked such elementary questions as, do you here voices? Do you believe in a higher power? Do you believe in angels? Have you ever seen angels? Etc., all of which I had to answer truthfully. Finally, I was in this one office and the psychologist asked me his questions. Right then, I determined that I had had enough! So I said to the good doctor, Sir, you and I have had several visits together, and each time it seems to be nothing more than a rehashing of what all was said previously. Tell me Doc, I see many of your plaques mounted on the wall behind you. You have some pretty impressive credentials and other doctorates and such, but let me ask you. Have you ever been in a situation where you had to act quickly to save someone's life? Have you ever had the occasion, where you had to pick up body parts or to wipe someone's brain matter from your person? Have you ever served our country in the military, and been exposed to combat? To each of these

120

questions, the doctor said, No! I then stated, Well doc, no offense intended, but it seems to me that I should be inquiring of you and your unqualified ability to evaluate me! In all practicality Doc, you and I have nothing in common and where you may have your book learning which you obtained in a closed protected classroom environment, I have acquired my credentials at the University called Life! Upon hearing this, the doctor stood up and demanded that I leave his office! I never saw him again.

Chapter 19
There Is Life after the Fact

"Consider the work of God: who can make straight what He has made crooked? In the day of prosperity be joyful, but in the day of adversity consider that God has made the one side by side with the other, so that man may not find out anything that shall be after him."
Ecclesiastes 7:13, 14 AMP

As a result of the supervisory harassment, I was forced into an early retirement at the tender age of only 37 years, which officially commenced on May 15, 1989. I had to fight for this pension, because Lt. Joe and the other sergeants worked very hard to destroy my life, depriving me of this income. Several weeks later, I received an invitation to meet Sergeant Dick at a local restaurant. With much caution, I did meet him. He sat across the table from me a broken man! His overall disposition revealed a humble side. He stated, Ed, I owe you an apology and I need your forgiveness for the things that I had done to you! You and I were friends and I allowed myself to be intimidated by the Captain and Lt. Joe. I asked, how so Dick? Sergeant Dick said, Lt. Joe used peer pressure on all of us and threatened each of us sergeants with a dock in pay, days off or a suspension if we did not lean hard on you! Upon hearing this, I stated, Sergeant Dick, do you know what you are telling me? You are only confirming that which I already knew in my heart, but I had no way of proving it!

We spoke of many things that had transpired between us during this 19 month ordeal. I accepted Dick's apology and I did forgive him. I also told him what Almighty God spoke to my heart eleven years previously on the plane, that I would not go a full twenty years towards a full service retirement with the CHP. We concluded our little chat and departed and I never saw Sergeant Dick again.

As I reflect back upon my law enforcement career at this juncture, I know that I've had several spiritual encounters, many of which are short stories by their own right. However, since it has been nearly two decades since I last had an occasion to speak of them, my memory of these encounters has been challenged. So in this chapter, I shall write of a few other testimonials, if only in a piece-meal or abbreviated expression.

For example, since I was no longer in uniform, I had opportunity to attend Sunday services. In the fall of 1988, I was approached by a woman at church. She said, Excuse me sir. Are you that CHP officer that Lt. Joe is harassing? I stopped and expressed my concern to her that it was none of her business. Apologetically, she begged for my attention as she said that she had a viable interest in this harassment! She went on too say, Officer Marr. I want you to know how sorry I am for you and your family. You see, Lt. Joe is my uncle and he was over at the house a couple of weeks ago for a family reunion. He became intoxicated and spoke of you and what he was doing to destroy you! This woman went on to say, I've wanted to inform you of this, but I missed you on Sundays, so I determined that if I saw you today, that I would do whatever to speak with you. You see brother, my uncle hates Christians with a deep hatred! Again, her comments to me only confirmed my hearts knowing of this reality.

Again, I received a dispatch call to respond to an irate motorist who had been involved in a multi-vehicle collision on I-5 south bound at the Palomar Avenue overpass in south San Diego.

Both Officer Al and I arrived simultaneously and approached the Chula Vista P.D. units already at the accident scene. The officers informed us that the one driver had been drinking and was very aggressive. Since the collision had occurred on the freeway, the CVPD officers assisted the CHP with scene stability with traffic control until we had arrived. Both Al and I walked up to this hostile man and without hesitation, I stood about 6 feet from him and with my arm extended towards him said in an assertive manner, In the name of Jesus Christ of Nazareth, I command you to shut up and come out of him! Immediately, this drunken fool dropped to the concrete like a bad habit! I instructed Al to cuff him and all the people around stood in place in wonder as to what they thought they had just seen.

Another situation involved a fellow officer whose older brother was a body builder. Apparently, this brother injured himself while training. The officer asked me earlier if I would consider visiting his sibling in the hospital as the officer had already spoken of me to his brother. So I, along with this officer, did visit this body builder brother. We exchanged our niceties and then I got down to business. The injured man accepted Jesus Christ as Lord and Savior and I found out hours later, that he had been healed of his injury! He was released from the hospital later that evening!

Again while working Bonita Valley, an up scale rural community, Officer Al and I responded to a possible suicide attempt on north bound Spring Valley Road north of Bonita Valley Road. It was late evening and the report we received was that a man had been seen jumping out in front of traffic. His actions caused one motorist to leave the roadway in an attempt to avoid striking the pedestrian. As we arrived and having confronted the pedestrian, I said to him, I command this spirit of suicide to come out, in Jesus name! Immediately he too dropped to the ground, at which time I was able to cuff him without further incident.

Then there was the time while I was at home. It was just past midnight, when I was awakened to the sound of many voices in my bedroom! As I lay there in my bed, I noticed several dark shadows (of men) seemingly standing shoulder to shoulder all around the three sides of my bed and facing inboard at me. They were heckling me saying, we are going to enter inside you and rip your body to shreds just like that little girl in Belize, (a country in northeastern Central America). I also heard frightening throaty sounds coming from the midst of them. Very much afraid, I buried my face in my pillow and prayed to Almighty God to come and save me from these tormentors. I repented of my backslidings and literally wept in my pillow. Here I was a CHP officer, who was accustomed to hooking and booking 300 pound bad guys, and I was weeping like a baby! It wasn't too long before I heard the foot steps of another approaching. Knowing that it was Jesus Christ coming to my aid, I was suddenly filled with strength and courage. I took the pillow from my head and sat up in bed. I said to these tormentors which I could still see, Okay! I'll show you who is greater! So I reached out as if to grab them by a shirt and pulled each one into my chest. With each one that I did grab, in their place was a void. I eventually grabbed all these tormentors and did compact them into a ball of sorts and threw them out the window. Interestingly, the closed curtains moved forward against the open window as though something had been tossed at it and through it!

Since 1989, I've had many jobs to supplement my pension. The reason for so many I suppose was due to a stigma that hovered over me as a former law enforcement officer. I've been laughed at! I've had interviewers get up and walk away from me in disdain! I've had some interviewers state, let's just say that we don't have a police department for you to supervise! Time and again, my attempts to support my family failed. The jobs that I had have been short lived or were very tenuous, at best. I eventually attended a vocational school, where I learned the basic skill of architectural drafting. After I graduated, I immediately opened for business, working for myself. I transformed my garage into my office, having purchased the slant board and all the appropriate drawing utensils and other templates that I needed. Although it was a slow start, I persevered and before too long, I had generated a few projects. Eventually my efforts paid off. I had acquired several clients which included other draftsmen and architects who were overloaded themselves. In all, I generated more income drafting then I earned working the beat!

I had planned a family trip to Ruskin, Florida in late July 1990 to visit mom and dad. Prior to my vacation, I completed all client responsibilities. While there, Saddam Hussien invaded Kuwait, Lebanon. When my family and I returned to San Diego on August 9th, I learned that his invasion caused a panic around the world! Suddenly, all the customers that I had before my vacation, vanished! I had no work whatsoever! As it turned out, many other draftsmen such as I also lost their businesses, and it seemed as if the world's economies were headed for the toilet! Literally, this global event forced me to look for work elsewhere. I tried to find employment with several P-Eye firms as well as attorney firms in legal art. Obtaining none, I did acquire some self-employment as a Bankruptcy Representative for a law firm out of San Francisco, Calif. In this capacity, I represented their creditor clientele in Trustee Court in downtown San Diego. It was my duty to reaffirm creditor loans from those citizens who had fallen on hard times. I really enjoyed this work, however through no fault of mine; I lost my employment due to an in-house collapse of the attorney firm in San Francisco. Finding myself looking for work again, I eventually found self-employment as a Traffic Violator School (TVS) instructor with the Sears Department Store. At the time, Sears was hosting TVS in many of their stores and these were contracted out. So I completed my battery of DMV driving examinations, and was given a teaching certificate. This credential authorized me to instruct the motoring public on the basic Rules of the Road. I found work as I said, and for the next 18 months I taught on weekends and two nights through the week. I enjoyed this work very much. So I entertained the notion of acquiring my own TVS so I worked very hard at accumulating the minimum hours mandated by the DMV. The cost was $2000.00 initially, but by the time I had acquired my hours, the basic annual fee soared to $8000.00! This unreasonable price hike left several TVS out of business, and only the most successful schools were able to survive! Before too long, I experienced problems with my voice. I went to the doctor and was told that little nodules had grown on my vocal cords. I was told to stop speaking! Once again, I had to overcome another of life's little hurdles. Consequently, I had to give up my instruction, due to medical reasons.

I could go on and on about other employments that I had, not to mention the months without! But suffice it to say that I was not a happy camper! My marriage ended as a result and I lost my family. I was a nervous wreck, in that I experienced a nervous breakdown as a result of all the stress. My doctor told me, Mister Marr, I don't want you to think that I am telling you what you should do with your life, but if you don't do something drastically different soon, something devastating will happen to you! Do you understand, Mister Marr? I knew what he meant. Later that week, my good friend Officer Al stopped by my home for a visit. We sat in my living room and weeping Al said, Ed, look at you! You are not the same man you were 6 months ago! Ed, you know what you have to do! I said, Al, I am not going to file for divorce! My son Ed Jr. needs me! Al replied, Ed, you are not going to do Ed Jr. any good if you are planted six feet under pushing up daisies! When I heard those words, it was as though I was hit in the head with a 2x4! I was stunned! Now, Al knew nothing of what my doctor had said, so I knew that I had to do something drastic, even that which I did not want to do!

Chapter 20
My Sojourn in Lake Havasue

"Yet I am glad now, not because you were pained,
but because you were pained into repentance [and so turned back
to God]: for you felt a grief such as God meant for you to feel,...
For godly grief and the pain God is permitted to direct, produce
in you a repentance that leads and contributes to salvation
and deliverance from evil, and it never brings regret:
but worldly grief (that hopeless sorrow that is characteristic
of the pagan world) is deadly [breeding and ending in death]."
2 Corinthians 7:9, 10 AMP

I include this unfortunate event in my life, because I wanted to show the tragic side of the stress caused by those circumstances beyond my control. Without going into all the imagined sequences of possible events, suffice it to say that I experienced a nervous breakdown that literally threatened to kill me! During the last quarter of 1995, I lost 50 pounds and through it all, I suffered with intense full thickness chest pain! I endured this pain round the clock for at least four months. My back had locked up and caused my left arm to become numb. My left hand grew very weak, leaving me with a 20 pound grip strength! I wept uncontrollably and the jitters besieged me, leaving me fearful for my very life!

I considered my failed 23 year marriage and my innocent 11 year old son, Ed Jr. I was forced into a situation, where I had to either act or die! So I filed for divorce in March of 1996. I moved into an apartment in Bonita Valley and then in June, I relocated to Arizona and resided in a desert community called

Lake Havasue, where I spent the summer. I rented a small one bedroom house. I had no neighbors other than the lizards and scorpions. The heat was reminiscent of my days in the Marine Corps where I served in Dhahran, Saudi Arabia as a Marine Security Guard. The hottest it became in Saudi Arabia was 137 degrees in the shade!

In Lake Havasue, I had no furniture, although I did rent a refrigerator and a bed. I bought a lamp, a small radio, and a plastic lounge chair. I essentially lived out of my suitcases and my vehicle! During this sojourn, I poured my heart out to God! My physical pain disappeared, although I still had the shakes. I placed a map of Texas on the wall of this house, as I've always had a desire to reside there.

After many days, the Word of the Lord came to me and nearly everyday after that and for many hours at a time, I pressed in with God. I felt so low and filthy! I allowed Him to conduct whatever He needed to do in my soul, to cleanse me. I allowed Him to perform those things He needed to do, knowing that intense pain would be the outcome. This pain of heart had been the years of accumulated junk from my past, both distant and the most recent! It was as though I was struggling against another man! Intuitively, I knew that other man; it was the old Ed Marr! Late on the third Tuesday night of August, 1996, I was awakened about 3:00 am. I walked out to the back patio, and reclined in my lounge chair. It was 115 degrees. Sitting there quietly, I sensed that the Spirit of God was near. So I said, alright Father, You spoke with Moses and all your prophets in the desert. Surely, you can speak to me. What is it? Immediately, I heard His audible voice, and that for the second time ever! My heavenly Father stated, my son, country western music has its hub in Nashville, Tennessee. I responded, yes Sir! He said, Silicon Valley is the hub of computer technology in America, is it not? I said, I suppose so. My Father then said, Washington D.C. is the seat of government for the nation of America, and every state has its own capital as does every county have its own county seat, do they not? I said, yes Sir! He then said, I too have a hub of ministry! It is Dallas/Fort Worth! The brooks of Cherith have dried up, the ravens are no longer going to feed you and I am sending you to Zarephath!

I was very familiar with this Scriptural account involving the Prophet Elijah, as found in the Book of 1 Kings, chapter 17. So I stated, Lord! You know I just came through a divorce and you know that I don't need another woman in my life right now, especially a widow! But nevertheless, Lord I will comply! Since it was still so late into the night, I returned to bed. Now this conversation occurred early on a Tuesday morning during the third week of August. I spent the rest of the week swimming or kayaking in the Colorado River. On Sunday, I attended morning services at Lake View Community Church for the first time, which means that I did not know any body there. The Pastor conducted the praise and worship from the stage, and afterwards he stepped down onto the floor. There were about 500 people in attendance and we all stood there in silence looking at the pastor. I sensed that he had something on his mind, and that he was pondering his thoughts. He then said the following. From time to time, the Spirit of God does speak to me in such a way that I am compelled to speak that which may be considered odd to many of you. But this morning we have a visitor, and it is to you sir, whoever you might be that I speak! And know this, that what I am about to say publicly, for you sir are your marching orders from Almighty God, Himself! Now, our Lord awakened you earlier this week and during the very early morning hours, you heard Him say to you: The brooks of Cherith have dried up. The ravens are no longer going to feed you and He would send you to Zarephath! My brother, I don't know what Zarephath may be or what it means, but know this! You did not imagine this conversation, but go in faith knowing that Almighty God has already gone before you!

As he spoke, I was so overcome with the reality of these words! I began to jerk violently standing there at my seat! I wept heavily, so much so that everyone knew to whom these words were intended! After the service, I introduced myself to this pastor. He embraced me, comforting my heart for he sensed that I was in distress. I thanked him for his words and he encouraged me all the more, even expressing a bit of envy for what all that Almighty God would have for me. The following Thursday, Sept 6th I departed Lake Havasue and headed for Fort Worth, Texas.

I arrived in Fort Worth on Friday afternoon, Sept. 7th about 3:15 pm. I did not know anyone! Once again I found myself in a strange land. I settled in for the night, at a local hotel and ordered a pizza. I had $276.00 to my name. I collected my thoughts and remembered a conversation I had with my pastor (J. Hanoum) back in Bonita Valley on Monday, June 20th of 1995. The previous day was Sunday, June 19th Father's Day. My pastor, at that time, hosted a ministry visit from an old acquaintance of mine, whose name was "Big" John Hall, whom I had known since October 1982. I remember this Father's Day, because of the dinner I enjoyed with "Big" John after the evening service. On Monday morning the 20th, I received a phone call from the church. The secretary informed me that a funeral was to be conducted at the church later in the day and the pastor requested my assistance! She indicated that several "undesirables" would be in attendance and that pastor needed me to wear a black suit and to stand guard as it were. I told the secretary, that I would come but since I am no longer in uniform, the only thing I would do, should something violent occur would be to call the police.

134

Fortunately, there was no hint of violence from all those undesirables and after the funeral service, my pastor approached me saying, Look at you Brother Ed! You look like "Big" John Hall! Ed, I want you to stop by my office before you leave for home. I have something I have to tell you, okay? So about an hour later, I did see the pastor. He said, Brother, the Spirit of God spoke to me early this morning and what I have to say may seem strange to you. Now Pastor Hanoum seemed awkward. He carefully chose his words and said, Ed, the Lord told me that He would be calling you away from San Diego sometime in the future. I don't know what that could mean, but He will send you to a desert. You will experience a wilderness trek that most people would decline. I don't know whether you will be called to full time ministry such as me or whether you will be involved in any ministry, in the traditional sense. But I do know what He told me. He said to me early this morning that he has called you. He has separated you, He has chosen you for Himself and that He will send you out into a wilderness where He will teach you things that the Body of Christ does not know; and then He will send you back and you shall teach us those things which we have never known! Ed, does this make any sense to you?

I told Pastor Hanoum, brother, at 3:30 this morning, the Lord did awake me. As I sat in my easy chair in prayer, there appeared before my eyes a pair of hands gripping a thick metal bar. These hands then snapped this bar and a brilliant flash occurred. In wonder, I sat there asking God what this meant. He then said, my son, I have called you; I will separate you, for I have chosen you! I will send you to a desert, and there I shall instruct you on things you have never known!

On Saturday morning, September 8th, I awoke to the sound of heavy rain. I polished off my pizza leftovers from the night before. After breakfast, I thought I'd do some exploring. I headed west on I-820. I saw a large church building, south of the freeway at Beach Street. What intrigued me about this building was that it seemed so familiar. Although I have never been to Texas, I could not help the fact that I have seen this building before! So I parked in the lot and walked around, even in the rain! Suddenly, it hit me! I returned to my vehicle and removed my cassette tapes. Pictured on the cover of one of them, was a much younger "Big" John Hall poised for a photo shoot in front of this very church portico! I thought, could it be that this is "Big" John's home church? I decided to wait around awhile. As it turned out, the church had a scheduled Saturday morning ministry event which I decided to attend. There were about 100 people in attendance. I met "Big" John's wife, and introduced myself. She indicated that John was out of town for the weekend, but that I could contact him after the weekend at his lube shop. Meanwhile, as I listened to the visiting minister, my thoughts were more focused on my current situation.

Prior to the morning events, I had already made a proposition with God. I said, Lord, you know that I don't know anyone here. For me to stick around any longer than 12 noon would be useless. So I will give you this morning to move on my behalf! If you don't, then I will head south to Lafayette, Louisiana and spend some time there with my sister, Darlene and Lord, you know I really don't want to do that!

At 11:30 am, we all broke for lunch. I was approached by another brother, who invited me for lunch. I accepted and for the next four hours, I told him of my current situation. He excused himself for a phone call. Minutes later, he returned and said that it was time to leave. He drove to an ATM and withdrew cash. He then turned to me and said, Brother Ed, I left the table to call my wife and I told her of the instructions the Spirit of God had given me. The Spirit of God had already spoken to me earlier this morn-

136

ing while in class. He told me to invite you to lunch and to listen to you. As you related all that you said, He told me to give you this $500.00. I don't want you to repay me, since this is not a loan. All I ask is that you tell no one that I gave you this money. Right then and there, Almighty God proved Himself greatly on my behalf! I knew that I was to remain in Fort Worth, Texas and there I did reside for another four years. I attended an Adult Bible School (Calvary Cathedral International, CCI) and graduated. Big John and I became good friends and He allowed me to be his armor bearer, in that I maintained his lawn during his ministry absence out of state, and during local ministry visits, he permitted me to become his chauffeur and his vendor on several ministry engagements.

Chapter 21
The Champion of the Lord

"I shall not die, but live, and declare the works of the Lord."
Psalm 118:17

I started to frequent CCI in October 1996. John Hall had suggested that I do so, since he knew that I desired more of God than what I was accustomed to receiving at the mainline denominational church. On December 26th, 1996 after the evening service at CCI, I walked to the very back of this cavernous sanctuary. Its dimensions reminded me of a shallow water tower. Its concrete walls rose 60 feet to meet the domed ceiling. The floor plan was circular with a seating capacity of 2300. Truly for me, this was the largest church I've had the pleasure to visit! I stood in the back of this spacious sanctuary, facing the pulpit which was back dropped with a huge stained glass rosette style circular window. Suddenly, the sanctuary was transformed into a huge stable! I no longer saw the sanctuary as it was, but I saw horses and chariots, some of which were harnessed together. I saw the tack on the timbered walls and could see the twitching muscles of many of these steeds. My thoughts became focused on the movie, Ben Hur. As you might recall, Ben Hur became the charioteer of a team of milk white horses, for the climatic chariot race. In the movie, Ben Hur positioned each of the four horses within the chariot harness, according to their individual strengths. He positioned the strongest, slowest horse on the inside, while he positioned the fastest horse on the outside of this harness. By doing this, the team best functioned most efficiently together in the race.

I asked the Lord what the significance of this vision was. He told me, there shall come a time in the not too distant future when there shall be ministry teams of at least two but no more than four. No longer shall a single man be the superstar! This vision convinced me to attend CCI regularly. I attended the Bible School in January of 1997. On January 5th, while in morning service, I met a little fellow named Nicholas K. He was a business man from Jacksonville, Florida and was in Fort Worth on business. He had decided to visit CCI and just so happened to be seated to my left. During the praise and worship, Nicholas, reached up and pulled on my left shirt sleeve, getting my attention. He said to me, Mister, I have a Word from God for you! Ignoring him, I continued on enjoying the awesome presence of God. Again, Nicholas reached up and pulled on my shirt sleeve, and again he said, Mister, I really do have a Word from God for you! So, to appease this stranger, I inclined my ear to him and listened. He began to speak. I was very startled by what he said, so I asked him to write this Word down on a piece of paper. He complied and this is what he wrote:

My son, I call you my champion! Just as David slew Goliath, you too shall slay the giants of this land! I have placed that champion inside you. Even your physical size is no accident, for I have made you a giant on the inside and out! Men will know that you are my champion because the sword of my Spirit shall be in your hands and my Words will come forth from your lips. Your light will shine bright in the land and it will drive out the darkness from within the hearts of all impenitent men! Rejoice my son, for I will be at your side just as I was with David and Moses!

(Presently, I have this Word framed in my home office, and it speaks volumes to me every time I read it!) In early January 1998, evangelist Tim Storey spoke to the Bible School students.

I was still in school at the time. He said much, but of all that he did say, one thing would be brought to my attention in a matter of weeks. Specifically, that on Sunday morning February 2, 1998, I arrived at church early for Sunday school. The class was dismissed early, so I went down to the sanctuary. I met some friends in the back row and I sat their enjoying our conversation. In time, people began to fill the sanctuary through the double wide swing doors that lined the very back wall. Soon, an 86 year old woman entered, in the company of the throng of people. This woman took perhaps four steps into the sanctuary and then collapsed to the floor! She hit the floor about 6 feet from my location. I immediately reached down and scooped her up in my arms and sat her lifeless body in the chair. Her body was very cold to the touch. Her tongue was jutting out of her mouth and there was no inhalation. I checked her pulse at her carotid artery as well at her wrist, and found none. People gathered all around, many of them weeping. I shouted out, Will somebody please call the medic and will some one look for a wheelchair! In the meantime, I spoke to this lifeless body. I knew that she had just passed on. I said to this body, Dear lady! Just who do you think you are to pass on without my approval! I mean, you have not even asked Pastor Bob for his consent! Just who do you think you are and where do you think you are going? I said, There is much still for you to do here. There are loved ones that will miss you!

Now I am a big man, although I am certainly not the largest. At 6 foot 6 inches tall and nearly 350 pounds, I felt the size of King Kong on this occasion! I mean, as I knelt there with this woman, my spirit was huge! I knew that it was the power of God welling up within me. I just had to withhold Him back until the proper moment. Finally, I belted out loud, this woman shall not die, but she shall live and declare the wonderful works of God, in Jesus name! As I spoke, all that power within and without me, some how was absorbed into my body and then surged powerfully through my arms into her body! Immediately, breath returned to her frail body! She lurched forward inhaling deeply. People rejoiced all the more. As for me, it was like a flash back to my uniform days. I said, Lord that was pretty neat! This lady walked out on her own accord, and was taken to the hospital for observation. Incidentally, the ambulance never arrived. Apparently, nobody bothered to call one when I had requested! Go figure! After this woman departed, one of my fellow Bible School students approached me saying, Ed, you are the one! What do you mean? I asked. Don't you remember what Brother Tim Storey said to the class? I guess not, I said. He said that there is someone in this class room right now who will raise the dead and that person will become God's greatest evangelist to this world today! I replied, Gee, I must have slept through that one!

Then on February 6th 1999, at about 11:30 am, I received a call from another acquaintance. His name was Gary. Gary was a car salesman, who worked at the Nichols Ford Dealership in South Fort Worth. I met Gary several months earlier, when I tried to trade in my Ford SHO for another vehicle. Anyway, on this date in February, 1999, Gary informed me that a coworker named Peggy had informed him that her daughter-in-law (Darla) had been admitted to the hospital for congestive heart failure, and that she had actually died on the operating table only to be resuscitated. So Gary told me that he had spoken of me to Peggy and asked me if I could visit Darla. So I asked Gary to patch me through to Peggy. I told him that I'd prefer to get her permission, before I do anything. Peggy answered the phone and I introduced myself. I said, Ma'am, this is Ed Marr friend of Gary. He just advised me of Darla's situation and so I am asking you for your permission to visit Darla. Peggy said, Oh Mister Ed! Gary has told me so much about you and the wonderful testimonies that you have. Yes! Would you please visit Darla!

At the time of Gary's call, I was serving court papers through-out the community of Fort Worth. Since I was close to home, I went there for lunch and to discuss this phone call with my new wife Sandi. It just so happened that I had just completed a manuscript entitled, The Aspects of the Audacity of Faith, which contained hundreds of faith ditties that covered at least eighty different scenarios of daily life. Sandi and I prayed up and after a few hours, I paid Darla a visit. I walked into her room. She was hooked up and was cognizant of my arrival. I said to her, Darla, you don't know me, but I am here by way of an invitation from your mother-in-law to pray for you! Now I don't really care why you are here, for I could take you up and down this corridor and show you other patients who are in worse shape than you! I told her, Darla, there are people outside these walls that truly do love you so much so that they allowed me a complete stranger to them and to you to pray over you! During the course of my intro, Darla showed no emotion whatsoever! Undeterred, I proceeded to pray over her, addressing her disposition, her physical condi-tion and her present spiritual situation. Darla then spoke saying, it is true. I did die over the weekend. They were operating on me and I left my body! I was met by a tall dark man, whose face I could not see. He took my hand into his and he led me down this lighted hall. At first, he seemed pleasant but soon turned evil. He grabbed hold of my hand, as I tried to pull away. We seemed to descend faster and farther down a darkened corridor. I cried aloud to God and then instantly I was back in my body!

I was very impressed by her claim. I said, Darla, I have not died as you had. Therefore, from my position, I have to accept that there is an after life by faith. However, you have been on the other side and you know first hand that there is life after death! So from this experience, you know more about the after life than

C. H. P. - Coffee Has Priority

I. So Darla, you must realize that your physical life is more than just clothes on your back and money in the bank, right? I then asked her if she would like to meet Jesus Christ. Darla said that she would, so I lead her in a prayer of salvation. I then asked her if she is content to sit here in this hospital with her failed heart. She said she preferred to leave. At this time I did pray over her body. I read several of my faith ditties to her and expounded upon them as the Spirit of God gave me the inspiration. Darla began to sweat profusely. I could feel the heat rising from her body. Several minutes went by. I asked Darla to tell me what she felt. She said, Mister Ed, I feel intense heat around my heart and it radiates throughout my body from there. I am very hot, but I am not burning up! I told her, Darla! That is the power of God healing your body! All that I said to you previously is but the substance of faith and the evidence of this faith shall be the result of a healed heart, which you are receiving right now! I left the room shortly thereafter. This occurred on Monday, the 6th of February. On Wednesday, I stopped by the Ford Dealership for a visit. Immediately as I walked in, Gary shouted, Mister Ed is here! Mister Ed is here! Every employee including the owner himself stopped what they were doing and ran towards me in a high state of joy! I assumed that something wonderful occurred. So I asked Gary what had happened. He said, Ed, you haven't heard? No Gary, I stated, I haven't been told. I was mobbed! I recall a nicely dressed black woman ask me if she could snip a lock of my hair for good luck! I was escorted up stairs to Peggy's' office. Gary pointed to me mouthing, He is here! Immediately Peggy dropped her phone and ran towards me in heels. She planted both feet firmly in front of me and leaped upwards wrapping her arms around my neck weeping tears of joy! Peggy said, Oh Mister Ed! Thank you! Thank you! Thank you! I was on the phone just now telling others of the wonderful miracle that had occurred as a result of your visit. This morning, I went to see the doctor at the hospital and to pick up Darla. The doctor told me, that they conducted another round of tests on Darla's heart as they intended to perform more surgery on her. To their amazement, they could not find anything wrong with her heart! They gave her a stress test, they pumped dye into her veins, they took her pulse, and everything and they could not find any disease! Darla is home right now completely healed! I have a brand new daughter-in-law and you have given me my son back!

Several days later I received a Thank You card from Darla. I still have this card and in it she wrote the following:

Mr. Ed,

Hello, just wanted to drop you a few lines to let you know how much the visit we had meant to me! It was one of the greatest times of my life! I thank you from the bottom of my heart! It was a great feeling and you know they couldn't make my heart go into spasms! It's a miracle! I thank God every day! So you can add my testimony to your list. Peggy brought me this valentine bear after you left. I named it Mister Ed. He stayed with me in bed the whole time! I'm doing better each day-I thank God again and again for that wonderful day! Thank you so very much it was so nice of you to come see me...

Love ya,
Darla Tankersley

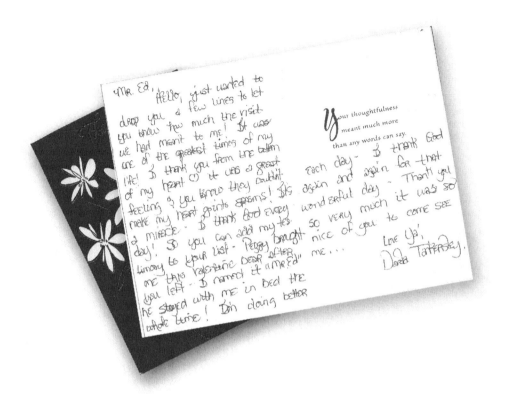

Mr. Ed, Hello, I just wanted to drop you a few lines to let you know how much the visit we had meant to me! It was one of the greatest times of my life! I thank you from the bottom of my heart ♡ it was a great feeling & you know they couldn't make my heart spirits spasms! It's a miracle. I thank God every day! So you can add my testimony to your list. Peggy brought me this Valentine bear after you left - I named it "Mr Ed," he stayed with me in bed the whole time! I'm doing better each day - I thank God again and again for that wonderful day - Thank you so very much it was so nice of you to come see me... Love Ya', David Tattersley.

Your thoughtfulness meant much more than any words can say.

Chapter 22
God's Charge and My Divine Assignment

"Thus saith the Lord of hosts,
If thou wilt walk in my ways, and if thou shalt keep my charge,
then thou shalt also judge my house, and also keep my courts,
and I will give thee places to walk among these that stand by"
Zechariah 3:7

In the summer of 1994 back in San Diego, a young lady from the church choir told me the following, Brother Marr, I was in the shower this week when the Lord spoke to my heart informing me that He has special plans for you. It seems that He will teach you things that the rest of us don't know! Does this make any sense to you, Brother Ed?

In March of 1996, I entered a Wal-Mart Super Center in Littleton, Colorado looking for work. I stepped up to the Customer Service desk and was greeted by a woman from behind the counter. She was standing there doing some paper work and without looking up at me, she said, Sir, I knew you before I met you! I said, Excuse me? She repeated herself and I said, Look lady! I just need some employment okay? Can you help me? This employee instructed me to walk to the Lay-A-Way Department at the rear of the building and someone there would assist me. Following her instructions, I waited to be called in for an employment interview. I waited a good hour and nothing! I was just about to leave when this eccentric woman from the Customer Service counter appeared and sat down on the bench beside me, eating a hamburger. Again she opened a conversation with me saying, you have a sister who lives in the south and you love to drive long distances! The Lord showed me in a dream earlier this week that a very tall man wearing a red/black flannel shirt and dark blue denims would stand before me at the counter and you are that man! She went on to say in essence, The Lord would have me to tell you that in the not to distant future, you will be addressing the nation and drive the darkness from the hearts of all men! People will be reading about you in newspapers, on Television and hearing you on the radio! So be assured that Almighty God has gone ahead of you preparing the way!

On a Sunday morning sometime in late 1997, as I sat in my usual seat at Calvary Cathedral waiting for the morning service to commence, a black woman (stranger) walked over to me and said, Sir, I have been impressed of the Lord to come over here to you and to tell you what He had just spoken to me. The Spirit of God instructed me to tell you that you are His prophet for this day and age and that you shall be used of God as one of His greatest evangelists this world has ever known!

On another occasion, while in class and waiting for school to begin, the Bible school assistant director approached me saying, Brother Ed, I just want you to know that God has informed me that you shall be a great evangelist in His service for these last days!

Throughout 1999, I was employed as a chauffeur in Fort Worth. On Monday night (January 11th) I had a 30 minute break between runs, so I stopped by CCI for a rare Monday night service. The guest speaker was Evangelist Steve Hill. Brother Hill has the distinct honor and the recognition as being used of God to initiate the Brownsville Revival in Pensacola, Florida. Now I have read extensive newspaper articles about this revival previously and this reading compelled me to be there on Monday night. On this particular night, he gave a message entitled, I Have Sinned!

CCI was packed out! There were an estimated 3500 people in the sanctuary, and the best standing position I could obtain was in the aisle. Watching my time, I knew that I would have to leave soon, but yet at the same time I knew deep down in my knower that Almighty God would have me to receive some spiritual thing at this service.

Printed on a large white poster board, which Brother Hill used, were the words, I HAVE SINNED! For emphasis, he took this poster board, thrusting his arms straight out towards the audience. As he did so, all present would shout out in unison, I HAVE SINNED! It had a powerful impact upon us all! Especially me! You see, as Brother Hill spoke, the Spirit of God said to me, Ed, does merely admitting I have sinned constitute true Godly repentance? I responded, I suppose not Lord, since you asked! The Spirit of God went on to say, Son, there are three things that shall move the hand of Almighty God in the affairs of men. They are Faith, Rebellion and Repentance, but necessarily in that order!

Upon hearing this, I knew right then and there that I had just been commissioned to embark on a wonderful journey, for I knew from past practice that whenever Almighty God speaks to me in this manner, He peaks my interests to investigate a particular topic. Immediately I set my mind and my heart to investigate Faith, Rebellion and Repentance. Seven years and six months later, having been sequestered from practically all traditional church activities, Volumes One and Two were completed. Volume one is entitled, Repentance: the Doctrine of God and the Knowledge of Salvation (in the Old Testament). It was published in August 2004 (See page 100). Volume two is entitled, Does Merely Admitting I Have Sinned, Constitute True Godly Repentance? Subtitled: Repentance: the Doctrine of God and the Knowledge of Salvation (in the New Testament).

Presently, all traditional ministry doors are closed to me, in that spiritual leadership across the denominational spectrum refuse to open their hearts and their pulpits to this Word of God's Righteousness for themselves and those who sit before them. So I have taken a different approach to publish this Word, namely through the newspapers. Since churches are closed to this Word, I have asked Almighty God to give to me a public platform. Give me this city, give me this county, give me this state, and give me this nation!

"And said unto them, thus it is written, and thus it behoved Christ
to suffer and to rise from the dead the third day:
And that repentance and remission of sins should be preached
in his name among all nations, beginning at Jerusalem.
And ye are witnesses of these things."
Luke 24:46-48

Epilogue

So here I am, driving this meat wagon to Balboa Naval Hospital. Talk about bells and whistles! This vehicle had it all. So I flipped every switch on its instrument board I saw as I departed. Good thing it wasn't a computer! With all the switches I flipped, had this ambulance been a computer, we probably would have all been deleted from off the face of the earth! We had about a 10 minute drive before we arrived at the Hospital. I allowed my thoughts to wonder about my life as memories flashed through the vast theater of my mind.

The Hospital entrance was in sight. Turning left from Pershing Drive, I proceeded up the hill towards the Emergency entrance, where a team of medics waited for our arrival. I pulled under the overhead and stopped. Immediately, the paramedics and the medical staff removed this young woman from the ambulance and wheeled her into the ER. I followed. As the medical team attempted to sustain her life, I stood at the foot of her bed and prayed over her broken body that Almighty God would repair this young woman's life and livelihood.

Thinking nothing more about her, I departed. I notified my radio dispatch that I was ready to be picked up at the Hospital for transport back to my patrol vehicle, which I had parked at the collision scene. I drove my vehicle back to the barn, completed my paperwork and secured for the night. I had two days off. Upon my return to work, I found a note in my office mail box (pigeon hole). The note instructed me that I was to call Doctor So and So at the Balboa Naval Hospital at my earliest convenience.

I called the good doctor and this is the gist of his conversation. Officer Marr? Yes sir! I am so glad you returned my call! I said, Doctor, Do you have something to tell me? Officer, I certainly do! Of course you remember the young college student that you brought in two days ago with the severe head and torso trauma? Yes sir, I remember. Well Officer, are you standing up or are you sitting down? I said, Doc! Just tell me what's going on! He said, Okay then. Officer Marr! Several of my team saw you standing at the foot of her bed praying. I said, do you have a problem with this Doctor? The doctor said, Hold on Officer Marr, please hear me out! You left and in your absence certain things occurred, which I thought should be brought to your attention. The Doctor went on to say, Officer Marr! I don't know what you said or what you did, but know this. What I am about to tell you, every member of my team wants you to know that a miracle took place right before our very eyes! I said, Doc! Tell me what happened! He said, you left and while the six of us where attempting to stabilize this woman, skull fragments began to pop back in place! Then her soft tissues within her skull were seemingly recreated before our eyes! Officer Marr! This woman was released this morning! She walked out of here under own power! What ever you said or did Officer Marr, all of us here at the hospital want you to know that we saw a miracle take place! Keep up the good work, Officer Marr!

This concludes my memoirs. I am compelled to state that many who read this book will consider my memoirs as ridiculous, even the fanciful dreams of a lunatic. Many folks I mentioned in part are in fact dead or have moved on to parts unknown to me. But despite this, I hope that my credibility has been established by virtue of the precise statements, the dates and the people involved.

Other Books by Ed Marr

The Aspects of the Audacity of Faith (Faith Ditties)
self-published July 2000

Volume 1
Repentance: The Doctrine of God
and the Knowledge of Salvation
(In the Old Testament)
Publisher-Xulon Press, August 2004

Volume 2
Does Merely Admitting "I Have Sinned"
Constitute True Godly Repentance?
Subtitled:
Repentance:
The Doctrine of God and the Knowledge of Salvation
(In the New Testament)

About the Author

Brother Ed Marr is an ordained lay-minister and published author. He is a graduate of Calvary Cathedral International Bible School in Fort Worth, Texas. Almighty God has groomed Ed as one of His Prophets (Right Reverend) to preach and teach Repentance as a true indicator of his authenticity as a true Prophet of God.

Lamentations 2:14 "Your prophets have predicted for you falsehood and delusion and foolish things. And they have not exposed your iniquity and guilt, to avert your captivity [by causing you to repent]; but they have divined and declared to you false and deceptive prophecies, worthless and misleading."

He is a retired California Highway Patrol Officer. His law enforcement career has taught him specific investigative skills, specifically the necessity for the economy of words. Ed's style of writing reflects this bare bones investigative technique. Prior to this, he served 7 years in the United States Marine Corps. His notable duties were as a Marine Security Guard (Saudi Arabia & Saigon) and a Drill Instructor (San Diego, Ca.)

God has used Ed throughout his law enforcement career. During his twelve year employment as a State Traffic Officer, Brother Ed experienced angelic visitations in his patrol car as well as at collisions. At crime scenes, Officer Marr has had demonic encounters, and as a uniform officer, hundreds have accepted salvation through the ministry Almighty God has called him to. Over the past thirty years, Brother Ed has experienced the power of prevailing prayer in that 3 people have been raised from the dead, and powerful creative miracles have occurred as a direct and immediate result of prayers of faith! Brother Ed has taught repentance to the prisoners at the Okmulgee County Jail where he was able to test the message of repentance, where frequently he received spontaneous standing ovations!

Ed believes that it is just a matter of time before the pulpits of America will open the doors to him and this NOW WORD of and about Repentance.

"Mister" Ed (as he is often called) is not another cookie cutter preacher who parrots others. His disposition is laid back, and his presentations are subdued. The very power of righteous words makes the impact, penetrating hearts, decimating carnality. (Job 6:25) Although a big man with a big voice, Ed does not rely upon these physical attributes to impress. Rather, he permits the fire power of The Word to express itself in truth!

While residing in Fort Worth, Texas, a specific prophetic word was spoken to Ed in January 1997, and the time has come for its fruition. That prophetic word is:

"My son, I call you my champion! Just as David slew Goliath, you too shall slay the giants of this land! I have placed that champion inside you; even your physical size is no accident! I have made you a giant on the inside and out. Men will know that you are my champion, because the Sword of the Spirit shall be in your hands and My words will come forth from your lips. Your light will shine bright in the land and it will drive out the darkness that resides in the hearts of carnal men! Therefore, rejoice My son, for I will be at your side just as I was with David!"

Presently, Brother Ed resides in Bixby, Oklahoma,
and he is available for field ministry. You may contact him at:

(918)574-5139
e-mail : *bigedvocal@gmail.com*